# American Indian Archery

*The Civilization of the American Indian Series*

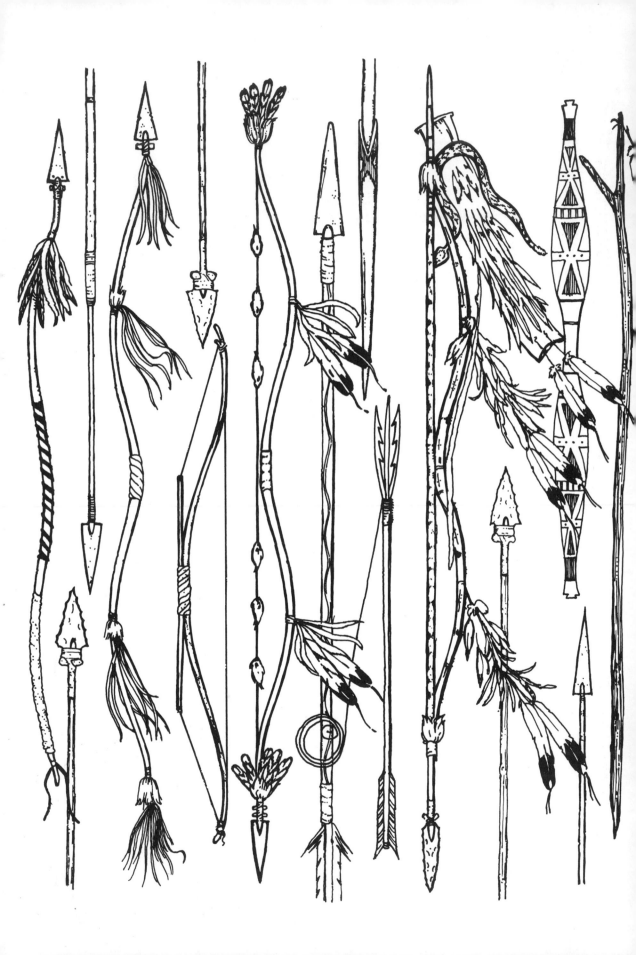

# American Indian Archery

## by Reginald and Gladys Laubin

Photographs by Gladys Laubin

Drawings by Reginald Laubin

*University of Oklahoma Press*
*Norman and London*

By Reginald and Gladys Laubin

Books

*The Indian Tipi: Its History, Construction, and Use, with "A History of the Tipi,"*
  *by Stanley Vestal* (Norman: 1957)
*Indian Dances of North America* (Norman: 1976)
*American Indian Archery* (Norman: 1980)

Films

*Indian Musical Instruments* (Norman)
*Old Chief's Dance* (Norman)
*Story of the Peace Pipe* (Norman)
*Talking Hands* (Norman)
*Tipi How* (Norman)
*War Dance* (Norman)

Library of Congress Cataloging-in-Publication Data

Laubin, Reginald.
    American Indian archery.

    (The Civilization of the American Indian series; 154)
    Bibliography: p. 175
    Includes index.
1. Indians of North America—Arms and armor.   2. Bow and arrow.   I. Laubin, Gladys,
joint author.   II. Title.   III. Series: Civilization of the American Indian series; 154.
E98.A65L38      739.7'3      78-58108
ISBN: 0-8061-1467-3

# Contents

*To the memory of the old warriors who revealed to us and taught us their lore of the bow and arrow.*

# *Illustrations*

## Color

*Black-and-White*

# *Foreword*

I have long considered writing about Indian archery, which has held a lifetime interest for me, to try and correct some of the misconceptions regarding this phase of American Indian life. If you are looking for a treatise on big-game hunting with bow and arrow, this will hardly be the book to read. If you would like to know something about the use of archery tackle and the ingenuity associated with its manufacture, and something about its importance to these first Americans, you will find new, valuable, and important information between these covers which should result in some of the pleasure for you that I have had in gathering the material. To me, it is not necessary to become a great hunter to enjoy thoroughly this ancient sport.

Although I have been acquainted with Indians for most of my life and practically consider myself one of them, having been accepted by many of them as a "relative," I have had little interest in hunting. Indians killed only out of necessity, and there has been no necessity for me to hunt. Many times I have been within a few feet of deer, elk, black bear, antelope, and once, before there were any restrictions on eagle hunting, a golden eagle sat on a pole right in my own yard. But how could anyone shoot such a beautiful guest? Since I pride myself on being a conservationist, I prefer to look upon the other game as friends also.

I have no quarrel with true sportsmen who obey the hunting laws and give the animals a fair chance. The real sportsmen do a great deal to ensure that we still have a game population. If the game animals were under no control, they could actually take over in some areas and in other areas could degenerate or starve because of inbreeding and overpopulation.

For my part I do not need the meat, and hunter friends supply me with skins, sinew, horns, antlers, or whatever animal products I may need. I prefer to see my animals alive. Elk, moose, black bear, coyotes, snowshoe rabbits, sage chickens, antelope, and even buffalo visit my wife and me in our own yard! At the same time there is a satisfaction in knowing that I have the tackle and the ability to get game if I ever need it. That is enough for me.

The biggest game I ever got was Gladys, my wife. She used to watch me shoot with the longbow, and Cupid eventually sent an arrow through her heart. She has offered no complaints when I have heated the house to ninety degrees or smelled it up working on horns, hoofs, rawhide, sinew, and glue. A wife who did not appreciate the value and final beauty of such materials could make life miserable for a prospective craftsman. I have been lucky in this respect, and I appreciate her loving care and consideration. Needless to say, this book would never have come into being without her continued interest and assistance.

# *Acknowledgments*

Gladys, my wife, first suggested that I write this book, and she has been of such great assistance that she is included as coauthor. I never cease to be grateful to her for giving me encouragement, inspiration, assistance with photography, drawing, and editing, and for the long research we have done together.

Nor can I adequately express my appreciation to Edward Shaw, Director of the University of Oklahoma Press, for his keen interest and encouragement after seeing some of my bows and learning that I intended to write something about them.

Many people have had an influence on my interest in Indian archery over the years. I wish to give special tribute to my old Indian "relatives" and friends, particularly to Chief One Bull, my Indian "father," Kills Pretty Enemy, Little Soldier, Philip Returns-from-Scout, Flying Cloud (Judge Frank Zahn), Mouse's Road, and Tahan. Tahan (Joseph K. Griffis), Kiowa, was one of the most interesting persons we have ever known. From his early life as a "primitive" Indian, later to become self-educated to the extent of reading in Latin and Greek, he lived a long and productive life of 105 winters. I am also greatly indebted to Nelson Hofmann, friend of the well-known bowyer, Robert Martin; to Dr. Ralph Hubbard, Director of the Indian Museum in Medora, North Dakota; Milford G. Chandler, collector for the Heye Foundation, Chicago Field Museum, and Cranbrook Institute; Dr. Harry L. Shapiro, Chairman, Anthropology, American Museum of Natural History; Dr. Andrew Whiteford, Director of the Logan Museum in Beloit, Wisconsin; Eldon Wolff, of the Milwaukee Public Museum; Vernon Erickson and John Norman Paulson, of the State Historical Museum in Bismarck, North Dakota; Ruth Butler, Curator of the Ayer Collection, Newberry Library, Chicago; Dr. Arthur McAnally, former Director of Libraries, University of Oklahoma; Charles Nedwin Hockman, Director of the Motion Picture Unit at the University of Oklahoma, for excellent and generous assistance with our photography; Dr. Frederick Dockstader, former Director, Museum of the American Indian, New York; Dr. Robert F. Heiser, of the Department of Anthropology, and William Bascom, Director, and Jerome Jenkin of the Museum of Anthropology, at the University of California at Berkeley; T. M. Hamilton, Missouri Archaeological Society; Jack R. Williams, Superintendent, Nez Perce National Park; Earl Brockelsby, Rapid City, South Dakota; Charles McCurdy, Chief Naturalist, Grand Teton National Park; Howard Johnson, Roy Martin, and Charlie Craighead, Jackson, Wyoming, and Steve Spencer, Idaho Falls, Idaho, never too busy to lend a helping hand; Nora and Virginia Snook, Billings, Montana, for locating hard-to-find prints; William Coperthwaite, Bucks Harbor, Maine, for Eskimo material; Philip and Vinola Newkumet, Norman, Oklahoma, for information on Caddo bows and arrows.

The interest and assistance of all these people have been deeply appreciated, and they have our warmest thanks.

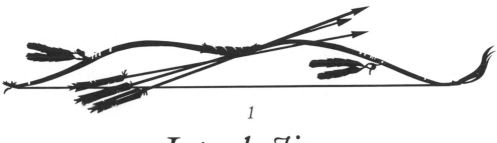

# 1

# *Introduction*

*So long as the new moon returns in heaven a bent, beautiful bow, so long will the fascination of archery keep hold of the hearts of men.*

Maurice Thompson, *The Witchery of Archery*

No one knows just when the bow and arrow came to America, but they were in use from the far North to the tip of South America when white men first arrived. Over the hemisphere the equipment ranged from very poor to excellent, and the finest bows of all were made in the Northwest of North America. Some of these rivaled the ancient classic bow for beauty of design and workmanship.

There are many who believe the bow to be quite recent in America, for there seems to be no evidence of it in the earliest cliff dwellings, although it does show up in later ones. It would seem to be of Asiatic origin but was brought over in later migrations, rather than in the early ones. The only sinew-backed, or sinew-lined, bows were found in North America, among Plains, Rocky Mountain, and California tribes. Some of these are quite similar in type to those found in parts of Asia.

The crudest bows come from the Amazon region, but even these natives took great pains with some of their arrows, which are almost as long as javelins.

The only place in the world where archery was unknown seems to have been Australia. That continent apparently was cut off from the rest of the world when the great ice caps melted and isolated that region before the invention, or discovery, of the bow and arrow. This is no proof that the theory of independent invention is erroneous, but the bow and arrow are far more complicated instruments than they appear at first glance. Those who are not convinced that independent invention took place find it difficult to imagine men all over the world independently stumbling upon them.

It is certain that the bow came nearest to perfection among the Turks in Asia Minor, but they brought the bow with them from deeper within Asia.

Some students believe the bow originated in Asia and thence spread gradually to the rest of the world. Its final development in various regions depended upon the culture of the people learning about it, its importance to their way of life, and the availability of materials, with even the weather playing an important part.

The bow seems to have been known among the Polynesians, but among them it was laid aside for obvious reasons: there was little bow wood available; there was no big game to hunt; and warfare, as among our Plains Indians, was a matter of personal contact rather than of destroying enemies at a distance.

Because I have always been interested in Indian archery myself and have found most of the popular conceptions about it to be erroneous, as are most of the preconceived notions about Indians, I would like to correct some of the false impressions and try to give a true picture of this ancient art as practiced by most of our original Americans.

Indian archery was quite different from the modern variety, or from English archery, from which the modern derived. The Indian archer has received a rather poor reputation over the years, and the further it is removed from its source the worse the reputation becomes. Indian bows and arrows have been pronounced inferior by the experts, and Indian shooting has been ridiculed as being very poor and inaccurate. I do not believe anyone has ever questioned the Indian's ability as a stalker and hunter, however, which after all are the important things when it comes to eating.

A legend once was prevalent that there was no archer anywhere in the world who could rival the American Indian. When the first European settlers arrived in America, archery was already on its way out in Europe. The settlers found Indians armed with bows and arrows dependent upon these weapons for securing game, the most important article in their diet, and for war. The natives excited the admiration of the newcomers with their skill in handling these important tools of survival, and the legends grew into feats hardly possible for even Robin Hood or William Tell to rival.

Generations later, with English archery once again coming into its own as a recognized sport, it became the custom to belittle the Indian archer. He used a small bow and short arrows, which could not possibly compare with the longbow and cloth-yard shaft of Old England. Furthermore, the Indian "deformed" his bow to shorten it still more, used heat on the wood, which was a sacrilege in England, and was accused of cutting through the grain on the back of the bow and of poorly tillering it. The former legend of great accuracy was now discounted, and it was decided that the Indian got so close to his game that he did not even need a bow. He could just push the arrow in with his hands!

Whereas the European first observed Indian archery during the decline of his own form, he began his derogatory comparisons with the revival of the longbow and the deterioration of native archery. Indians in parts of the East gave up the bow and arrow long ago in favor of firearms. The Iroquois laid aside the ancient weapons as early as 1727 according to Lewis H. Morgan. The guns of that period actually were inferior in most respects to the bow. They had longer range, and the rifle at least had somewhat more accuracy, but they were clumsy, heavy, and had a very slow rate of fire. An archer could discharge an entire quiver of arrows during the time taken to load one shot in the famed Kentucky rifle. Even this famous weapon often misfired, putting its owner in further jeopardy. The noise frightened the game for hundreds of yards around; so it was one good shot or an empty stomach for the firearms hunter. It is not unusual for a bow hunter to get two or even three shots at an animal if his first shot misses.

So why did Indians give up the bow so early? I think it was largely a matter of prestige. Like almost everyone else, they liked new things. The gun at first terrified them with its fire, smoke, and noise, but when they found they could obtain them for themselves and could handle the monsters as well as could the light-skinned newcomers, they were anxious to have them. To add to their lure, guns were very expensive, costing many pelts, which in themselves were not easy to obtain. Therefore, the man who could afford a gun was a special hunter, an exceptional trapper, and most important, an admired warrior.

In parts of the East, however, the ancestral weapons survived, or at least were reinstated. The Indians of Canada and Maine and the Cherokees of the South found the bow and arrow better for hunting after all. To this day the Cherokees use it because it makes no noise and because the Indian hunter can get the game he considers legally his without alerting game wardens, who take a dim view of aboriginal rights.

In the West too the bow began to give way to the prestige of the white man's mysterious iron thunder stick (*mazawakan,* or mysterious iron, in Sioux). But until the availability of the repeating rifle the majority of Indian hunters clung to the bow. Its easy availability and rapid fire made it a superior weapon, especially for buffalo hunting. They were not dependent upon white traders for bows and arrows. They were dependent for guns and everything connected with them, and guns were very difficult to get.

Detractors still insist that this did not make the Indian an archer, for he rode alongside his quarry almost close enough to touch it and could kill it as readily with a spear or lance—which he often did when out of arrows. But what about his taking deer, elk, mountain sheep, and mountain goats with arrows, which he did continually? Even though he was a superb stalker who knew all the characteristics and idiosyncrasies of the game he pursued, it was next to impossible to get closer than twenty-five or thirty yards from such game. Does this make him any less of an archer? Modern archers, with fancy bow-quivers and all the newfangled gadgets, plus all the ingenuity they can muster, make most of their kills at an average of thirty yards. And by far the majority of them come home empty-handed, which seldom happened to the Indian.

I had my eyes opened many years ago. I had been brought up first with the legend that the Indian was the greatest archer in the world, who could perform all sorts of uncanny feats; then, after being introduced to English-style archery while still only a youngster, I heard the other legend that Indians were great stalkers but could not hit the side of a barn unless on the inside.

On one of my first trips to the Standing Rock Reservation in North and South Dakota I took my own archery tackle along and asked some of the old-timers to try it out. It was the period when the English longbow was giving way to the so-called "Indian-type" flat bow. Most archers I knew were then using bows of about five feet eight inches in length instead of six feet. I had gone even shorter, using a five-foot bow made of Osage orange.

My Indian "father," Chief One Bull, ninety years old, known in history as one of the fighting nephews of Sitting Bull, and his old crony Kills Pretty Enemy looked my tackle over and remarked that it was a good bow, although much too long, as were the twenty-six-inch arrows.

I handed One Bull six arrows and placed a cardboard box about a foot square at a distance of approximately thirty yards. The old man held five arrows in his bow hand, *points up,* raised the bow to the sky as he looked at the target, then swiftly brought the bow down, drawing the arrow at the same time, and let go. The arrow missed the target by several inches. He did not draw to the head but to about three inches from it. He shot the other five arrows in rapid succession. All of them missed, but when I went to gather them up, they were all in one little cluster.

"U-i', u-i'!," he called out. "Not very good," he said in Lakota, "But you should have seen me when I was a young man!"

I handed him back the arrows and asked him to try again. This time he put all six arrows in the box. How he laughed! Then he sang a little song.

"How long since you've shot a bow?" I asked.

"More than sixty winters," he answered.

Imagine shooting a bow that well, a strange bow and strange arrows, after not having a bow in your hand in over sixty years! In addition his eyesight was not too good, and the box was the same color as the ground.

Later I learned that the average Sioux arrow would draw about twenty-three inches. A man measured his arrow length from the outside of his bent elbow to the tip of his middle finger, plus the distance from his big knuckle to his wrist bone. I have Sioux arrows of from twenty-two to twenty-six inches drawing length, but twenty-three inches was average. Bows were measured from the tip of the left middle finger, with the arm stretched out to the side shoulder-high, down to the right hip joint, with the bow held diagonally across the body. This resulted in a measurement of about forty-seven or forty-eight inches on the average. Sometimes the Sioux measured a bow merely to the waist, which accounts for some bows being only forty to forty-three inches long. These exceptionally short bows were usually sinew-backed (sometimes referred to as sinew-lined).

On another day we had another shoot with One Bull and Kills Pretty Enemy. This time we put a piece of paper about the size of a playing card in a split stick at about twenty yards. Both of these old men (Kills Pretty Enemy was eighty-seven), using my tackle, consistently hit the paper about two out of three times.

I was reminded of a story Dr. Robert Elmer told in one of his books on archery. He said that while he was vacationing in Canada an Indian came to see him one day who had heard that Elmer had a bow and arrows and so had come to show him how to shoot. Of course Dr. Elmer was amused and interested. As I recall the story, he had been playing solitaire at a table in the yard, so he picked up one of the cards and set it off about thirty yards. He braced his bow and handed it to the Indian with a couple of arrows. Quick as a flash he put both arrows through the card.

Elmer was amazed and, hardly believing his eyes, asked him to do it again. And he did do it again. So Elmer was satisfied that this Indian could do all right at short range. But on a standard four-foot target at forty yards the Indian had arrows all over the outside edge. He said the target was too big.

I imagine most Indians would have done poorly on standard targets beyond forty yards. But does this mean they were not archers? After all, they lived by the bow and arrow, but there was little or no purpose in becoming proficient at farther than forty yards. Making a high score was unimportant and to them uninteresting. The important thing was to feed the family and to protect it against enemies.

Among Plains Indians the bow was largely a defensive weapon in war because the only honor a man could earn was for touching an enemy hand to hand. Even if he shot an enemy at a distance with an arrow or bullet, he still had to touch the body to claim his honor. So there was no real reason to shoot accurately at a great distance. The Indian is a practical person. He does things in certain ways because he gets results.

Boys practiced shooting at butterflies, birds, rabbits, and other small game. They also played a game that was like pitching pennies except that they used arrows. One would shoot an arrow ahead, at any distance he might choose, and the others would try to hit it. The one coming closest started the next round.

Atsina (Gros Ventres of the Prairie) boys had a game in which they used a horn-shaped object made of long grass and bound with sinew. They stuck three long sticks, or arrows, in the ground in a transverse line a few inches apart and tried to hit the center stick with their arrows. In a close decision the distance from the arrows to the stick was measured with another stick, and the one whose arrow came closest had the privilege of throwing the grass horn in the air and trying to hit it with an arrow before it fell to the ground. If he did hit it, he won the game and was paid in arrows by the losers. The game was played until someone did hit the grass horn.[1]

Another favorite target was a moccasin thrown in the air, and many became proficient at shooting a tuft of grass while riding by on horseback at a full gallop. Does it take more skill to hit a nine-inch bull's-eye at eighty yards? I doubt it. The latter requires control and skill, but hitting such a small target as a tuft of grass only a few feet away from the back of a racing horse requires not only skill but expert horsemanship as well. I know because I have tried it. Also I used to set up three bales of hay, pin a small target in the center, and try to hit it as I galloped by. After I had tried this a few times, each time riding on past a short distance, reining in my horse, and turning around to walk past the target to pull out the arrow, the horse would do it automatically—slow down, turn around, and walk back to the target. While I pulled the arrow out, he helped himself to a large mouthful of hay.

To the Plains Indian speed and dexterity were important, perhaps as important as accuracy. Even though accuracy was developed mainly under forty yards, the bows evidently were capable of throwing arrows a considerable distance.

Dr. Saxton Pope made a study of Indian bows and arrows which is still cited to this day, but I am convinced that his tests were biased and even unfair. He was a longbow man and could not believe anything could surpass the glory of English archery. The English came down through history as great archers, and rightly so, but this does not necessarily mean they had the world's best equipment, or even that their method of shooting was the only right way. It has since been proven that the short bow, properly made, is far superior to the longbow in speed and trajectory; it will shoot farther and with a lower point of aim. So the Indian has one joke on the modern archers: for all their slighting remarks about Indian bows, the best bows we have today are more like Indian bows than the famous longbows of old. Although the bows of today are mostly longer than the Indian bows, they are shorter than longbows, flat, and have the recurves known to many Indian tribes which were formerly laughed at by the traditional English-style archers. No one has yet come up with a bow to equal the short, light, composite bow of the Turks, which averaged forty-five inches in length.

The justification for the longbow lay mostly in its easy manufacture and "sweet" shooting. An efficient short bow of equal power requires ideal materials and much painstaking craftsmanship, as well as a different technique in shooting which is harder to master.

There are few good American Indian bows to be seen today. The best ones were buried with the warriors who used them. Occasionally a beautiful specimen is to be seen in a museum, but most of the Indian bows in existence today were either inferior in the first place or have been made so by bad handling.

As I recall Pope's tests, his flight tests using flight arrows sometimes were under 100 yards. The best bow he used cast a flight arrow 210 yards. This is pretty poor shooting and would give the impression that even good Indian bows were inferior weapons. If he used bows like some that I have seen in museum storerooms, it is a wonder he got as much range as he did. I have seen a few bows that were beautifully made, but they were invariably in very poor condition because they had been cared for by people who knew nothing about them. Some were still strung after all these years. Others, in fact most of them, had been standing up, probably ever since they were first collected. I have seen several once-beautiful, highly reflexed sinew-backed bows which were broken because they had been strung backwards by some uninformed museum attendant. You can try to explain such a bow to one who knows nothing about them until you are blue in the face, and he will just think *you* are ignorant or crazy. I have pointed out bows strung wrong to several museum officials. I have gone back ten years later, and the bows were still strung wrong.

When anyone wants to see my bows, I have to stand guard to make sure he does not try to bend them the wrong way. One chap, who claimed to be a great bow hunter, picked up my most highly reflexed bow and started to put the string across the two tips, remarking that it "followed the string" very badly. I grabbed it from him just in time and strung it for him. Was he ever surprised! He made some lame excuse about not noticing that it was a reflexed bow, whereupon he proceeded to draw it all the way back and let the string snap. Some hunter! Fortunately the bow did not break, but anyone who knows anything about the care of archery tackle knows that one does not draw a bow and let it snap without an arrow on the string. The extra weight and friction of the arrow are just enough to keep the string from breaking and to prevent the consequent breaking of the bow itself. Nor should one allow a bow to be left strung or standing, but one lays it down or hangs it on a peg.

Some archers use a gun rack for their bows, but at Gladys's suggestion, I made a rack by putting two poles across the two logs supporting the ceiling in our bedroom. She said she wanted to see their beauty first thing in the morning, and when she awakes they are right there over her head. Last count, she said, was thirty-two bows.

I made a copy of an old Sioux bow, backed it with sinew, and with a sinew string shot an ordinary twenty-three-inch roving arrow 220 yards—better by 10 yards than Pope's best shot with an Indian bow on which he used a linen string and a flight arrow. Mine was a 5/16-inch roving arrow, cut down to twenty-three inches. The sinew string was the best the Indians had, but it is not nearly as good as linen (or dacron). In a table showing Pope's records the bow he used for his best shot was Yaqui, 59 1/2 inches long, and drew seventy pounds. Elsewhere he gives the impression that few Indian bows drew more than sixty pounds, but there are authenticated reports of Eskimo, Alaskan, and Yukon bows drawing seventy pounds, and I believe that other Indian bows were at least that strong, judging from the proportions of the bow that I copied in comparison with some others that I have seen but not handled.

My "Sioux" bow draws about fifty-five pounds at twenty-three inches and is of hickory, forty-eight inches long. Hickory is not rated as too good a bow wood; so I do not consider my little bow exceptional in any way, and I am no flight shooter. I made another "Sioux" bow, only forty inches long, this time patterned after one made by an Oglala named Eagle Hawk. It is half round in cross section—round on the back, flat on the belly—the worst possible shape according to some authorities. It is of green ash, a variety of white ash (not green in the sense of being unseasoned). It is highly reflexed and rather thinly backed with sinew, drawing about thirty-five pounds at twenty inches. With it I shot a bobtailed target arrow 179 yards.

Pope got only 153 yards with a flight arrow from a similar Blackfoot bow of forty pounds drawing weight. His best bow, the Yaqui, was of Osage orange, rated by many as the very best bow wood. Pope's tests have been pronounced by some to have been complete and thorough, but perhaps you can see why I do not consider them so. I do not feel that he even used average Indian bows, let alone the best. Nor did Pope ever mention the marvelous elasticity, even after laying idle for many years, of some of the bows he used. He drew a little forty-one-inch Apache bow twenty-two inches, a forty-inch Blackfoot bow twenty inches, a forty-four-inch Navajo bow twenty-six inches, a fifty-four-inch Yurok bow twenty-eight inches! Few modern bows would stand such overdrawing. Certainly the English longbow, of which Pope was so fond, would never stand it. The average longbow of six-foot length drew a twenty-eight-inch arrow.

Today there are few Indians who have ever had a bow in their hands. While archery is becoming an ever more popular sport among other Americans, Indians have been taught to regard it as a mark of savagery, and until recently most of them would rather be caught dead than with a bow and arrows. Nevertheless I had one interesting and amusing experience at Little Eagle, South Dakota, some years ago. Old Louis Dog had made a number of bows to sell in the local trading post. He came to see me one day, telling me he had heard that I was interested in bows and arrows and wanting me to buy some of his. His price was twenty-five cents for a bow and one arrow. Now, while they were not excellent bows, the old man had spent a lot of time on them, and they were certainly worth more than that. I told him he ought to charge more for them.

That afternoon some Indian boys were watching me shoot with my own tackle, of course, and wanted to try it. They did not do any better, or worse, than anyone else who had never tried it before. They wanted to know if I would make them some bows and arrows, so I told them to go and see Louis Dog—he already had some to sell.

The next day half a dozen of these little fellows came around, all armed with Louis's products. I asked them how much he had charged them for their new weapons. "One whole dollar!" was the response. This price had included a bow and three arrows. I was probably responsible for early inflation on the Standing Rock Reservation.

I do not know how long the "new" fad I introduced lasted, for although this was at the time when the official government policy had changed to encouraging the Indians to retain the best of their own culture, there were still some people in the Indian Service who did all they could to discourage anything Indian. But this I do know: recently, coinciding with the new interest Indians are showing in their own heritage, a few have once more gone in for archery. But not Indian archery! They have had no contact with real Indian archery for several generations. No, they are using the most modern equipment—fiberglass bows with all the accoutrements: balance weights, sights, mechanical releases, fiberglass or aluminum arrows. The only thing Indian is the archer!

Years ago, before 1924 when Indians were made citizens of their own country, an Indian had to go through the same procedures to become a citizen as any foreigner with a little ceremony added that was supposed to impress him with the grandeur of passing from savagery to civilization. He was handed a bow and an arrow and instructed to shoot it for the last time, far into the distance. Then his hands were placed on the handles of a plow, and he was told this was a good thing to push along.

Formerly Indians always made an effort to retrieve their arrows, but in this case the arrow was probably retrieved by one of the government officials, who kept it as a souvenir of his efforts to enlighten the ignorant savage.

As a paradox of history, which records that civilization developed after man gave up the chase to become a farmer, the Plains Indians developed their highest culture when they gave up farming to move onto the prairies to hunt the buffalo. They made greater changes in their methods of living in one hundred years than the rest of the world did in several thousands.

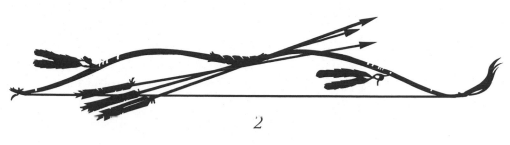

## 2

# History

*The moon gave us the bow, the sun gave us the arrow.*

Pawnee legend

Early illustrators on the East Coast—French and English—show Indians of the region with longbows that look identical to English longbows. I have always questioned whether the bows were actually like this, or whether the artists drew bows as they were accustomed to seeing them at home. Some of the drawings show bows which even look as if they had horn tips, as the best of the English bows had. Other drawings show recurved ends, and at least one picture shows a longbow with recurved tips and double-curved limbs. The double-curved bow is usually considered typical of the Plains Indians, but it is possible that tribes in other areas used it too.

Jonathan Carver's *Travels Through the Interior Parts of North America,* written about his experiences with the Sioux from 1766 to 1768, contains an illustration of a double-curved bow, apparently made of horn, but it also must be an example of artistic liberty rather than a representation of a true Sioux bow, for it is identical to the bows found in early Grecian art. It looks anything but North American Indian.

There is no doubt that the bows of the Woodland Indians were longer than those used in other parts of the country. Those in museums today are around five feet in length, some a bit longer, some a little shorter. The oldest and best known of these is the "Sudbury bow" in the Peabody Museum at Harvard University. It was taken from an Indian in 1660, and museum officials list the bow as Wampanoag—the people who greeted the Pilgrims. It is about sixty-seven inches long, made of hickory, and its cross section is identical to that of recently constructed wooden bows of the most scientific design arrived at by engineers striving to develop the most efficient pattern. It would seem to

Atsina grass "horn" target.

indicate that at least one Indian bowyer had learned to make a really fine weapon. There is no comparable Indian bow to be found today in any other museum, but this does not mean that there were not many more in earlier days, when white men were scarce and bows were plentiful.

One writer mentioned that the Sudbury bow "followed the string" to some extent and thought this was because it might have been left strung for a considerable length of time, but anyone acquainted with hickory knows that this tendency to follow the string—to remain somewhat bent even when unstrung—is the main fault of hickory wood. It is very tough and durable but soon loses its life, or cast, and is not considered too good a bow wood by real craftsmen. But it was the best to be had in some localities. Backing such a bow with sinew, however, not only improves the cast but completely eliminates string follow.

A wooden bow between five and six feet long is the easiest to make, does not break too easily, and performs well for the man on foot. Since, as mentioned earlier, most of the Eastern bows were about five feet long, this size no doubt proved to be best for use in the forest, being long enough to handle well and not too long to be a handicap while moving through the timber and underbrush.

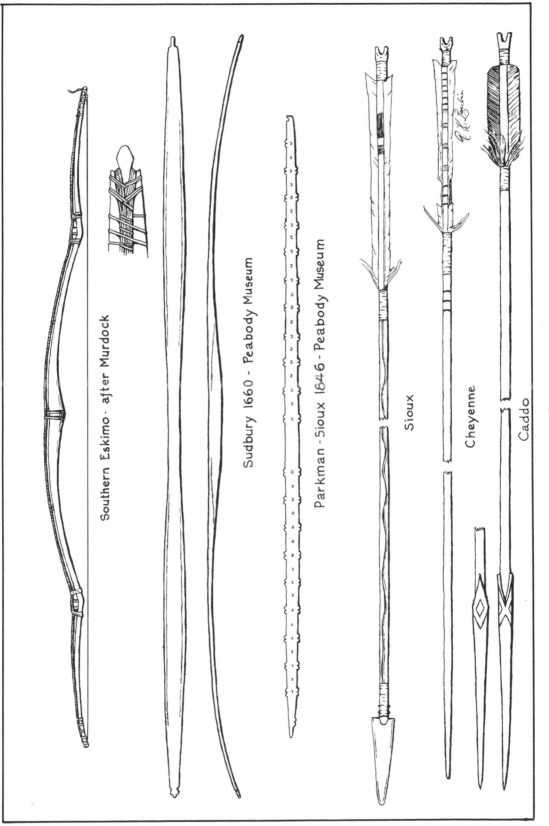

Southern Eskimo - after Murdock

Sudbury 1660 - Peabody Museum

Parkman - Sioux 1846 - Peabody Museum

Sioux

Cheyenne

Caddo

Bows and arrows.

Some of the English explorers were well impressed with the Indian archery they saw. Captain John Smith reported that they could "shoot levell" at forty yards and very near the mark. Such a bow was a good bow indeed, for only the stronger English bows would do as well.

Master George Percy, who was also in Virginia in the early 1600s, remarked that a "savage" put an arrow a foot or better through a target (that is, a leather shield), but when he tried an arrow against a steel target the arrow was shattered.

Another explorer stated that Indian bows were fashioned like English bows but without nocks; the string was run through a hole in one end and tied fast at the other. Which makes the pictures we have mentioned, showing decided nocks, more of a puzzle.

Columbus reported that the Indians had bows as large as those in France and England, with arrows one and a half to two yards long. The hard wood foreshafts were a span and a half and poisoned. Some arrows were tipped with fish teeth. These Indians were the warlike Caribs, who sent such a shower of arrows at Columbus's landing party that it hastily retreated back to the ships.

Six-foot bows were also found among Indians on the Gulf Coast by the Narvaez expedition, which turned out to be a complete fiasco. Only the famous Cabeza de Vaca survived to get back finally to Mexico. Ten soldiers were transfixed by arrows although they wore armor, which shows something of the power of the Indian bows. The Spaniards learned about Indian archery the hard way.

South American bows range from 6 1/2 to 8 feet in length among the forest tribes, with some as long as 12 feet. Bows of tribes in the open country of the Pampas are from 52 inches to 65 inches in length. This seems strange, for the Indians of the Pampas did not use the bow on horseback, and it would seem that the shorter weapon would be more suitable on foot in the jungle.

The chronicler of the De Soto expedition wrote:

They never remain quiet, but are continually running, traversing from place to place, so that neither crossbow nor arquebuse can be aimed at them. Before a Christian can make a single shot with either, an Indian will discharge three or four arrows; and he seldom misses of his object. Where the arrow meets with no armour, it pierces as deeply as the shaft from a crossbow. Their bows are very perfect; the arrows are made of certain canes, like reeds, very heavy, and so stiff that one of them, when sharpened, will pass through a target. Some are pointed with the bone of a fish, sharp like a chisel; others with some stone like a point of diamond; of such the great number, when they strike upon armour, break at the place the parts are put together; those of cane split, and will enter a shirt of mail, doing more injury than when armed [wearing armor].[1]

In the second volume of the narratives it says, "The Indians, on two occasions, killed three soldiers of the Governor's guard and wounded others, and killed a horse; and all that through bad arrangements, since these Indians, although they are archers and have strong bows and are skillful and sure marksmen, yet their arrows have no poison, nor do they know what it is."[2] Up to this point the expedition suffered 760 injuries from arrows.

De Soto took an Indian prisoner and had him demonstrate the power and accuracy of his shooting. He pierced a coat of chain mail at 150 paces. A second coat of mail was then placed on top of the first, and an arrow pierced both of them but did not go completely through as it had the first time.

At first the Indians were afraid of the expedition's horses but laughed at the crossbows and muskets. They soon learned that the horses were more vulnerable than the riders; so they killed the horses first and then dispatched the men as they struggled to get to their feet. Even Spaniards wearing plate armor were killed by shots through the eyes, mouth, and throat, and were wounded in any place unprotected. It did not take them long to learn that metal armor was not the best protection against Indian arrows. They discarded most of it and made a quilted armor instead.

Near present-day Mobile, Alabama, Rinjel, one of De Soto's officers, withdrew "more than twenty arrows" from his armor made of a loose coat quilted with coarse cotton ("Egyptian cotton" is native to our Southland). The Indians were well acquainted with it, and the Spaniards would have had no trouble getting it at the right season.

Further on we read that Don Carlo's horse was shot in the breast with an arrow. When he dismounted to withdraw it, he was shot in the neck and was killed almost instantly.[3] Then we learn that soon after this 22 Spaniards were killed and 148 others were wounded. There were 688 arrow wounds in all. Seven horses were killed, and twenty-nine wounded: "The arrow shots were tremendous, and sent with such a will and force that the lance of one gentleman named Nuño de Tovar, made of two pieces of ash and very good, was pierced by an arrow in the middle, as by an auger, without being split, and the arrow made a cross with the lance."[4]

Three horses were shot through both shoulders with arrows. These could not have been propelled by the sort of little children's bow we so often see as being "real Indian."

One Indian attack was repulsed not by the Spaniards but by the weather. A "tremendous shower" wet their sinew bow strings, rendering their weapons useless, and they turned back.

In the three and a half years of the expedition between 1539 and 1543 they lost two hundred fifty men and one hundred fifty horses from arrows. But, heavy as their casualties were, and for all the efficiency of Indian archery, the invaders on one occasion destroyed a village of five thousand people, killing them all. The military organization of the newcomers, coupled with their great use of treachery, enabled them to attack friendly natives and to win the advantage in many instances. In the end, however, the expedition crumbled as had Narvaez's before them. The men who were not killed by Indians died of starvation and disease, and the remnants of the party escaped to Mexico as best they could.

The French also found good reasons to fear Indian archery in the South. On an expedition to Florida in 1565 only forty of their soldiers were left unhurt. Again, finding that arrows were ineffective against plate armor, Indians shot at faces and legs. Cabeza de Vaca reported a range of two hundred yards for Indian arrows and said that they could pierce an oak as thick as a man's thigh!

In 1540 the Coronado expedition came up through the Southwest and as far north as the plains of Kansas. Castañeda wrote that a Teya (Apache?) shot a bull through both shoulders with an arrow, "which would be a good shot for a musket."[5]

In later historical accounts of the Plains, Belden (quoted in Clark's *Indian Sign Language*) said that he had found a man's skull pinned to a tree; the arrow had pierced the entire head and penetrated the tree far enough to hold it in position, apparently for a number of years. Bourke, writing of his experiences in the Apache wars, said Apache arrows were effective at one hundred fifty yards and that in 1871 he saw a pine tree pierced six inches by two arrows. I doubt that he meant that the pine tree was six inches in diameter. Rather, it was probably a small pine sapling, and it would be perfectly possible to pierce it with an arrow from a strong bow so that the arrow projected six inches on the far side. Bourke had a friend killed by an Apache arrow in the chest, and the arrow had a wooden foreshaft but no other point. Mason quotes Maltebrun as saying that Apache arrows could pierce a man at three hundred paces!

Even if some of these stories are somewhat exaggerated, the chances are that Apache bows were much stronger and more efficient than any that Pope tested. His Apache bow drew only twenty-eight pounds and shot a flight arrow a mere 120 yards. He said the bow was of hickory, but where the Apache got hickory, unless from some part of a white man's wagon, would be a mystery.

I remember as a boy hearing a story of an Indian hunter who shot an arrow completely through a buffalo cow and killed the calf on the other side of her. There are several authenticated incidents of hunters driving arrows completely through buffalo so that they stuck in the ground on the other side. My old friend Chief White Bull claimed to have accomplished such a feat on four separate occasions.

Since there is no doubt that originally there were many Indian bows of considerable power, let us now take up some of them in more detail.

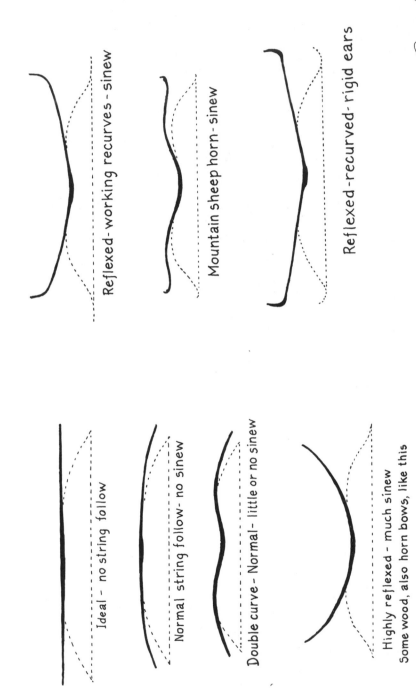

Reflexed - working recurves - sinew

Mountain sheep horn - sinew

Reflexed - recurved - rigid ears

Ideal - no string follow

Normal string follow - no sinew

Double curve - Normal - little or no sinew

Highly reflexed - much sinew
Some wood, also horn bows, like this

Bow shapes, relaxed and strung.

## 3

# *Comparisons of Bows*

We have already mentioned the longbows of the East and Southeast and that some bows of the latter area have been reported as long as six feet. In at least one drawing a longbow with double curve was shown. This is probably an accurate representation, as the double-curved bow does not seem to have been used in Europe, at least in recent historic times. The classic Cupid's bow known to ancient Greece was doubtless made of horn. It must have been backed with sinew, for horn alone does not stand the tension necessary for a bow. Later, bows of horn and sinew were known to other countries of Europe in the shape of the crossbow, before the development of steel crossbows. The steel crossbows usually had recurved tips; somewhere along the line this improvement in bow design was developed. Since it was known much earlier to Oriental and Asia Minor bowyers, it seems somewhat strange that the principle was not applied to the horn-and-sinew crossbow as it was to the steel. Suffice it to say, most of Europe, before accepting the crossbow, was content with a short wooden bow without sinew. This bow was inferior to the longbow because it was not possible to bend such a bow enough to make for efficient or powerful shooting.

There are some old prints which show English longbows with recurved tips, but perhaps these were merely the whim of the artists influenced by the ancient tradition of short reflexed and recurved bows. From the literature and traditions that have come down to us regarding English archery, it apparently was considered foolish and detrimental to heat the bow stave in order to accomplish either a reflex or recurve. It is possible that the English made an occasional bow of two billets joined at the handle, in which case the bow could easily be reflexed and would provide some insurance against string follow. But it is the exceptional self bow (and even a joined wooden bow of this type is a self bow in my category) that does not have at least a slight string follow. Because of the tradition mentioned above, it is doubtful that English longbows were ever recurved.

However, we now know that recurving the tips of a bow gives a decided improvement to the cast. The resulting "ears" act to shorten the working limbs of the bow and act as a lever to aid in its drawing. The resulting action is far springier and faster. Indians in the Woodlands discovered this principle long before white men arrived, and many of their bows were recurved at the tips. Even in recent years, with practical archery long gone from their lives, they have made little tourist bows with recurved tips. One Seneca bow in the Albany Museum, which is about fifty-eight inches long, has a long recurve on each limb, a hole drilled through each limb about eight inches from the tips, and the nocks are cut slanted toward the back rather than the belly of the bow. The string goes from the nocks through the holes in bracing the bow. I can see no advantage in such an arrangement, although there may be some. It would seem to make the ears inactive. But an Indian usually had a reason for doing a thing, although sometimes that reason was ceremonial or aesthetic and not practical to a modern way of thinking. Someday perhaps I shall make a bow like that to learn how it really behaves.

Another Seneca bow is ornamented with scallops all along one edge, while still another (see drawing) is scalloped on opposite limbs.

The principle of the ears was known also to the Eskimos, to some Canadian tribes, and to the Northwest Coast, Plateau, California, and Desert tribes. Even a few Plains bows have slightly recurved ends, but often these are due to the tension of sinew backs. The little horn-and-sinew bows also often had slightly recurved limbs. Many bows, however, from all these areas were turned up at the tips merely for looks; the ears are so short as to have practically no effect on the shooting. Some are even above the nocks.

In New England, hickory and white ash seem to have been preferred, where available. But in Maine, where neither of those trees grows, they used hop hornbeam (ironwood) and red cedar. These two woods occasionally were used in other parts of New England too, along with sassafras and witch hazel. However, John Josselyn, writing in 1674, said that walnut was preferred. To this day people in Connecticut call hickory "walnut" (wall nut?); so perhaps this is what Josselyn meant, because there is no black walnut there, and white walnut (butternut) would seem to be a very inferior wood. The Beotuk Indians of Newfoundland were reported to have used sycamore.

James Adair wrote in 1775 about the Cherokees, "They make perhaps the finest bows, and the smoothest barbed arrows, of all mankind."[1] Mason, quoting Timberlake's writings of 1765, said the Cherokees used oak, ash, and hickory for their bows. They liberally coated their bows with bear oil, warming them before the fire to increase the penetration of the oil. The Iroquois to the north as well as Algonquians were credited with using the same woods. There was no mention of either black or honey locust, but from our experience with the Cherokees in recent years, they preferred those locusts. Most of the Cherokee bows that I have seen are about five feet long, of flat, rectangular cross section, 1 3/4 inches wide above the handle tapering to 3/4 inch at the nocks, double notched at each end, usually with rather pretty diamond-shaped tips. They now make them reduced at the handle to about an inch wide, but the older bows were only slightly reduced. Some of the bows that they still make, even some of those made for tourists, are very well made, would draw better than fifty pounds, and are really very efficient weapons.

In the Cherokee range of Timberlake's time there may have been some ash available, but there is no white ash that I know of on the Qualla Reservation today. They made strings of twisted bear gut and possibly of woodchuck hide, which is very tough, as their Iroquois relatives did.

Le Page du Pratz said the Natchez made bows of acacia, first with bark strings, later with strings of hide.

The tribes around the Great Lakes used somewhat shorter bows. Whether these tribes near the border of the plains were influenced by Plains Indian bows is hard to say, although most Plains tribes came originally from the East and shortened their bows when they took to the horse. It is possible, then, that the Great-Lakes-area bows were also longer in earlier days like other Woodland bows.

I have seen a Chippewa bow that was about forty-seven inches long, and Walter J. Hoffman reports forty-six inches as a typical length for a Menomini bow. The Chippewa bow had a single notch at either end; both notches on the same side. Menominis preferred hickory for a bow, with ash as a second choice. Occasionally they used a sinew backing, but at one time they made a very fine compound bow—an ash back and cedar belly glued together, with a sinew layer, or lining, on the back covering even the sides of the ash, wrapped with sinew at the grip, at the ends, and usually at a couple of places on the limbs in between. The Menomini bows were coated with deer brains as a measure of protection from moisture and to keep the wood from becoming brittle.

In making a bow the wood was heated by the fire, which softened it a little and made the working of it easier. The measurements of one hickory bow were 46 inches in length, 3/4 inch thick by 1 1/4 inch wide at the center, tapering to 5/8 inch at the ends. The cross section of the bow was rectangular. The nocks were 1 inch from the tips. The string was of sinew from the back of a moose. Menomini bows were strung in the manner of Plains bows, which we shall take up later. Some Menomini bows were scalloped on the left side (the archer's left), apparently for decoration, although such decorations could have aided in aiming. Every Indian I have heard of shot instinctively rather than using a point of aim, but I believe that even an instinctive archer uses a point of aim, even if not consciously.

The Menominis are among the few tribes credited with using poison on their arrows, dipping the tips in rattlesnake venom. Hoffman, writing of the Menominis, said it was "safer to stand before an Indian's rifle at eighty yards than at the same distance when he was armed with bow and arrow."[2]

Crossing the Missouri River we find the Omahas using bows of ash and ironwood and occasionally of elm. They did not seem to care for hickory, although it grows in their area. They said that ash and ironwood did not warp when exposed to wet weather and that the best wood of all was from an ash killed by a prairie fire. The best time for cutting green wood was in the Moon When the Geese Return, or February. The wood was then hung by the fire until it was time to work on it.

At one time the Omahas attached a long blade to the upper end of the bow so that the weapon could also serve as a spear. Alice Fletcher reports that their bows were slightly reflexed at the center and that the upper limb bent more than the lower. Most bows made within the last fifty years bend slightly more in the upper limb because that limb is made from 3/4 of an inch to 1 1/2 inches longer than the lower limb to achieve better balance. Perhaps the Omahas had discovered the same principle.

Most Indian bows, however, seem to have had the handle at true center, which means that both limbs were of equal length and the arrow was held above center. While many archers are of the opinion that a shorter lower limb gives better balance, I have made several bows with limbs of equal length and find no difference in shooting qualities. Perhaps a difference would be more evident in a longer bow. Many Indian bows made with equal limbs had the handle wrapped below center, however, so that the arrow did cross the bow at true center. The Turkish bow had equal limbs, and its performance has never been surpassed.

The Omahas used two notches in the upper limb and one in the lower limb for the string. Alice Fletcher said that the slip knot was placed in the upper notches and the string tied fast at the lower single notch. If her observations were correct, this would be the opposite of their other Siouan relatives, who when notching their bows in this fashion, tied the string to the double nock and used the slip knot on the single.

Francis La Flesche, who aided Alice Fletcher in her work among the Omahas, reported that the Siouan tribes seldom used the sinew-backed bow, considering it a "female bow," beautiful but too delicate, that would not stand weather, and so on. Educated Indians like La Flesche often knew little of the actual lore of their people until they returned home from school and learned it later in life. With a name like La Flesche (*la flèche* is French for "the arrow"), one might think he knew something of bows and arrows, but this does not seem to have been the case. (It is interesting that Fletcher means "arrow maker" in English; so we had the "arrow maker" and "the arrow" working together as anthropologists who did very valuable work in recording the history of the Omaha, Osage, Ponca, and Pawnee tribes.) In fact, the sinew-backed bow was preferred by most Plains tribes, including the Sioux, if not the Omahas.

The sinew bowstring on any bow could become worthless in the rain, but unless a sinew-backed bow is soaked in water for many hours the sinew certainly would not come off, and the bow actually would lose little of its cast. As additional protection from the weather the bows were always kept greased, and some had snake skin glued over the sinew as still further protection.

When Omahas did make sinew-backed bows, they used burnt mica to whiten the sinew after applying it. White clay was used by some tribes. But the mica, clay, or other agent used to make the sinew white was not applied between the layers of sinew, as one recent writer stated. No one who has ever worked with sinew would make such a statement. It was sometimes applied to the surface of the newly laid sinew while the glue was still wet, in order to make it stick and dry with the sinew, but to put it between layers of sinew would prevent the sinew itself from sticking and would ruin all the work. The main purpose of any of these whiteners was decoration, although it also could serve to prevent the glue from becoming tacky in wet weather.

Some Indians rubbed red ochre or blue paint on the wet surface instead of white clay or mica, but for the same purpose—decoration. After the back was thoroughly dry and the bow had been tried out for awhile, deer brains, bear grease, or other fat was usually applied to serve in lieu of varnish. West Coast Indians used the white clay as a background for the beautiful designs they painted on their bows.

Although, as among most tribes, any man was capable of making a usable bow, the Omahas had special bowyers who were acknowledged masters of their trade. A man who wanted one of their bows had to approach such a bowyer ceremonially with tobacco and gifts to get his consent to make it. The bowyer did not make arrows or strings. These were crafts belonging to other tradesmen.

Pawnees made bows of Osage orange, and of course the Osages used this wood. Its very name comes from them. The Osages say the moon gave the bow to the people and the sun gave them the arrow (the new moon and the sun ray). Accordingly, many of the Plains tribes regarded the bow as feminine and the arrow as masculine.

Bows and arrows were carried in many rituals and ceremonies and are still used ceremonially by a number of Pueblo tribes. Only recently we saw the Buffalo, or Animal, Dance of the Santo Domingos, and one of the "hunters" carried a beautiful bow, double-curved like Plains Indian bows, in an elegant mountain-lion-skin quiver. In some instances bows and arrows were made especially for certain ceremonies and were used in no other way. This may explain some of the very highly decorated bows we see or hear about and could be a reason for some bows being made of elk horn, buffalo ribs, or other materials which may not seem to be very practical.

A bow and arrow also played an important part in the *Heyoka* ceremonies of the Sioux. The bow in this case represented the sky, and the arrow the lightning. The *Heyokas* were Thunder Dreamers, known also as the Clowns, for they "did everything backward." Consequently, the bow in such rituals was usually merely a bent stick with a string on it, and the arrows were deliberately made poorly and crooked to carry out the theme of the ridiculous.

There was probably a good deal of individuality within any given tribe as to the length and strength of bows. Pawnees have been reported to have had bows from forty-eight to fifty-six inches long. And I have seen Arapaho and Navajo bows so near alike that it was difficult to tell the difference. They lived entirely different lives in very different parts of the country. Both bows were of rectangular cross section, sinew-backed, quite highly reflexed, and double-curved. But another Navajo bow I remember was half round, forty-five inches long, flat on the belly with the pith showing, sinew-backed, and wrapped with flat sinew strips at four different places. The last three bows mentioned all had double notches at each end.

From this same region but from the Hopis is a double-curved bow with double notches at each end, forty-five inches long, but with an oval cross section. Neither Navajos nor Hopis could be considered strictly horse Indians, but both had these short little bows.

Although it is necessary to use a short bow on horseback, this apparently was not the only reason for making short bows. We find short bows in a number of regions where horses were almost unknown. Most of the desert Indians, for instance, used very short bows, but this may be partially due to the limitations of the material available. Then again, some of the horse Indians used longer bows than we would expect. Parkman brought back a Sioux bow in 1846, now in the Peabody Museum at Harvard University, which is fifty-four inches long and straight. It is almost black, probably from age, neatly carved on both sides of both limbs with little projecting knobs, and has a line of brass tacks down the center (see drawing).

I have several little bows made by John Sitting Bull (the famous chief's deaf-mute son) and by Eagle Hawk, an old Oglala. They were made to sell at the local trading post, which in turn sold them to tourists. However, they were too strong for children's bows, and most tourists never appreciated them; so I bought the whole batch the trader had on hand.

Although these bows are all Sioux, and all of ash, the designs and workmanship of the two men are entirely different. "Deefy's" bows are from 40 to 43 inches long; most of them 41 inches. Most of them have quite a decided double curve, are about 1 3/8 inches wide by 5/8 inch thick at the grip, 7/8 inch wide by 1/2 inch thick at the tips, and are rectangular in cross section. There has been a great deal of criticism about Indian bows not following the grain. All these bows follow the grain very well, even though this is not an important consideration when a bow is backed with sinew.

Eagle Hawk's bows are all about 41 inches long. They are about the same size at the center as Deefy's, but taper to 1/2 inch at the tips and are nearly half round in cross section. This is supposed to be the worst possible bow design, but if one wants to bend a sapling to make a hoop or whatever, the best way to ensure against breakage is to split it, leaving a flat surface along the pith, and to bend it with the flat side in, the round side out. This may not make the most efficient bow, but could help to prevent breakage.

The same kind of bow when backed with sinew becomes a different weapon. When highly reflexed it is still further improved. Some Navajo and some Crow bows used this same cross section.

As another example of differences in bow making within one tribe and one community, John Sitting Bull's bows were always double notched on the lower end and had a single notch on the upper end on the left side. Eagle

Hawk's bows have a single notch on each end; the lower one on the left, the upper one on the right.

Eastern Sioux used hickory for bows. Western Sioux, in addition to ash, used choke cherry, wild plum, and crab apple. I have been told that Sioux also used serviceberry for bows, but it is about the worst wood I have ever tried to work, or at least our mountain variety is. The grain is crooked and twisted for the entire length of the stave. To work such a stave with bone and stone tools must have been an almost impossible task. It is difficult enough with modern tools—not even a table saw cuts it well—and we are reduced to more primitive tools such as rasps and files. Deefy's bows have plain, unwrapped handles, and his bows are painted, probably with water colors. A typical one has brown all around the ends for about four inches, a green belly with red cross stripes, and a pale red back. Eagle Hawk's bows all have handles encased in black broadcloth, spirally wrapped with heavy twine. The backs are rubbed with red ochre; bellies are natural color with red zigzags on each limb.

Although, generally speaking, it is easier and more pleasant to shoot with a bow that has a narrowed handle, one can shoot accurately from a wide-handled bow, the *archer's paradox* apparently taking care of it. The "sight window" on the modern bows, to my way of thinking, is a monstrosity, unnecessary, and ugly in appearance. It is another one of dozens of sales gimmicks.

Some Indian bowyers mastered the trick of canting a bow just enough that the string lined up closer to the left side of the bow, serving the same purpose as the sight window but without its ugliness.

I have a Cheyenne bow made by Mouse's Road of Osage orange that has a single notch on the right side of the upper end and two on the lower. Some writers have stated that it was always the *lower* limb that had the single notch, but obviously this cannot be true. This Cheyenne bow has a little spur carved on the single-notched end, just as an ornament. If the bow were braced with this end down, the spur would be broken off. Mouse's Road shot the bow with the spur end up.

Many Indian bows have a single notch at one end. This was common throughout the West. It is the end in which the noose of the bowstring is placed, and it is easier to slip the noose out of one notch than out of two notches.

Much has been said about the worthlessness of Osage sapwood, but this Cheyenne bow is mostly sapwood and shoots very well, even though it bends too far out on the limbs. It is fifty-two inches long, slightly double-curved,

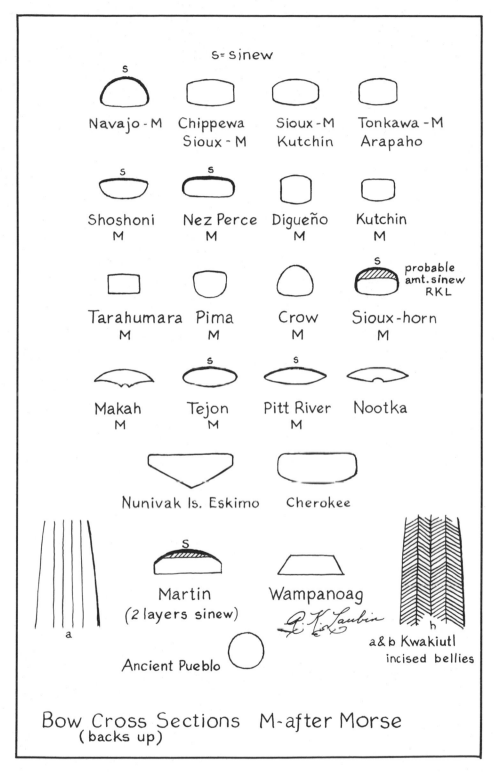

Bow cross sections (backs up). From Edward S. Morse, "Ancient and Modern Methods of Arrow Release."

and the curves nearly straighten out, or become one, in stringing the bow. Strangely, the bow does not kick. It has what amount to short working limbs on a long handle, or center piece, like many modern bows.

An ancient bow from the Pueblos, found not long ago in Lone Mountain Cave on Cameron Creek in southwestern New Mexico, is in the museum in Flagstaff, Arizona. It is 53 1/2 inches long with a round cross section, about an inch in diameter at the center, and tapers to 1/4 inch at each end. There are tiny little nocks for the string near the tip of each limb.

The Apaches of the Southwest are mentioned many times in articles and papers pertaining to Indian archery. Since there are several divisions of Apaches, it would be natural to expect to find some variety in their bows. All the Apache bows I have seen in various museums across the country were highly reflexed and double-curved, with sinew backs, from 42 1/2 to 44 inches long. But Bourke, who was with the Apaches in the 1880s, says that they seldom used the sinew-backed bow,[3] as does Morris E. Opler in speaking of the Chiracahuas, so perhaps both are right if speaking of this division. But, I repeat, all the Apache bows I have seen have been sinew-backed, and most of them are wrapped with sinew at the ends. Some are also wrapped spirally in addition to the sinew backing. Opler says the Chiracahua bows have the wrapping only. He also says they used the augmented pinch grip on their arrows, whereas the Apaches generally used the Mediterranean release (they were among the few North American Indians who did).[4]

The White Mountain, Warm Spring, and Huachuca Apaches used *corded sinew* on their bow backs, like the Eskimos and some other peoples of the North.[5] Apaches, being Athabaskan, may have retained this as a tradition from their sojourn long ago in Alaska and the Northwest. Apache bows I have observed were strung in what I call the Cheyenne manner, which will be brought up later. Their bows were made of mountain mulberry and occasionally of cedar, and they were rubbed with deer or bear fat. One bow I remember was dyed dark blue except for the handle, and it had only one notch on the upper left side and two on the lower limb, like many Plains Indian bows. Some Apache bows had no nocks except those built up of sinew.

Paiutes and Chemehuevis of the deserts sometimes made compound bows, probably using mesquite, mountain mulberry, or mountain mahogany for the back and juniper or cedar for the belly. A hardwood was commonly used for the back and glued to a soft wood for the belly, with a layer of sinew over the back. This is one case where I think it would be proper to use the term *lining* instead of backing for the sinew, because the hardwood would truly be the back and was thicker than a mere core. These were small bows, only about three feet long, and Cupid-shaped. However, I usually call the sinew a back, or backing, for even a thin layer of it can add as much as ten pounds to the drawing weight of the bow. The Chemehuevis sometimes covered the sinew lining of the bow with a rattlesnake skin, with the rattles still attached as an ornament.

Lewis and Clark said the Shoshonis made bows of cedar and of pine, but I cannot believe that pine would do for a bow. Spruce, perhaps, but it would be pretty poor stuff, except with a heavy sinew backing. Or the "pine" may even have been yew, which was available in the western part of the Shoshoni range. These bows were only about 2 1/2 feet long and were pronounced of the same shape as bows used by Sioux, Mandans, and Minitaris (Hidatsas). They said the Shoshonis also made bows of elk horn and of mountain-sheep horn and that the latter was most highly prized. They preferred otter skin for quivers.

O. T. Mason said the Blackfeet did not make bows of antler or horn, but it would seem strange if they did not because they lived in the same type of country and had the Shoshonis for neighbors. Catlin said that the Blackfeet and Crows both had horn bows.

Mason also said the Blackfeet traded as far south as the Arkansas River for bois-d'arc (Osage orange), and I would not doubt this.[6] They were known to raid as far south as Mexico. But he also said the Blackfeet are Siouan. The people we usually think of as Blackfeet are Algonquian, and in recent times they have lived in Alberta and Montana. There is a division of the Sioux Nation known as Blackfeet (Sihasapa), a branch of the Teton, now living around Kenel, South Dakota, on the Standing Rock Reservation, but I can find no information of any Sioux ever using Osage orange.

The Nez Perces, also near the Blackfeet, and the Crows, who have been friends of the Nez Perces for a long time, made beautiful little horn bows. They made small wooden bows too of similar length, thirty to forty inches, heavily backed with sinew, and highly reflexed. Unstrung they looked like a shallow letter C. A friend of mine years ago owned one of these little bows, which he believed had belonged to Chief Joseph. Be that as it may, some "ignoramus," he said, had strung it backward and tried to shoot it. This was the first time I had seen a bow that had been broken in this way.

The Klamath Indians of Oregon also made short bows of yew, about 3 feet long and 1 1/2 to 2 inches wide. They were made from green wood, the sinew was applied while still green, and they were hung up in the sweat house until cured. With these short bows the Klamaths used a 30-inch arrow, although it is doubtful that they drew them to the head. Some of the California tribes are also reported to have made bows of green yew, curing them in the sweat house.

California, extending more than eight hundred miles along the coast, is of course a state of many climates and was inhabited by many tribes and sub-divisions of many stocks. While we usually think of the short wide bow as being typical of California, there were really many varieties to be found through-out the state. In the southern deserts bows were made of the "root of wild willow" more than six feet long.[7] I never knew any root could be straight enough for a six-foot bow, but this is what Mason said. Could they have joined two pieces? Willow and even cottonwood are supposed to have been used by some desert tribes. These woods, which grow near water holes, are about the only woods there that are long enough for bows of any kind. The Yuroks, a western branch of the great Algonquian stock located on the coast in the northern part of the state, made some bows only 33 inches long, as much as 3 1/2 inches wide, and only a quarter of an inch thick—quite a contrast to the five-foot bows of Algonquians in eastern and northern parts of the country. The Maidus, farther inland and a bit to the south, made bows four feet long and about 1 1/2 inches wide, while the Hupas, who were in between, made bows of green yew as much as 59 inches long. It is hard to find yew that long; yet their bows were not of two pieces joined at the handle. But the Hupas are an Athabaskan group, so perhaps it is possible there was still some tradition of the longer bows of the north.

Many of the California bows had nicely recurved limbs, and most were quite highly reflexed. Some, like the Miwoks, added small recurved tips of sinew that served only as ornament. Others were recurved only a couple of inches, also mostly as an ornament, but some were recurved for six or eight inches, which would add cast to the bow. Makahs, like some of the Northwest Coast tribes such as the Nootkas farther north, sometimes left a high ridge down the center of the belly of the bow, carving away the wood in *concave* fashion on each side of it, and then cutting a groove down this center ridge. They may have gotten the idea from the pith sometimes exposed in making a bow from a half-round sapling and decided to make a decoration of it. Some Nootka bows have a curved, or *convex,* belly with a groove along the center. Some Kwakiutl bows have the bellies carved in rather intricate line patterns.

The wide bows like those of the Yuroks are always narrowed somewhat at the handle to make holding easier and are sometimes called "paddle bows."

Ishi, the famous "last of the Yahis" from the vicinity of Lassen National

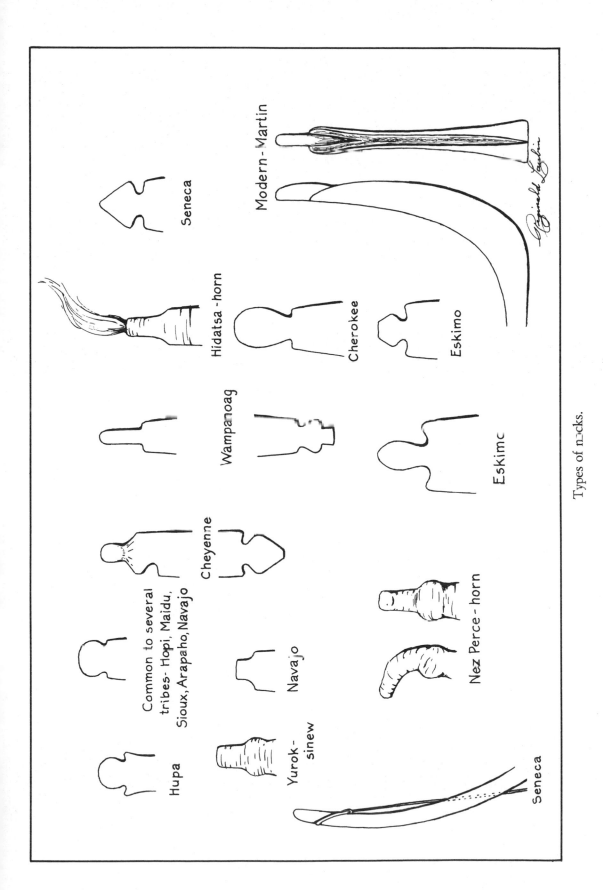

Types of necks.

Park, made his bows from branches of the mountain juniper. The end of the stave which had been next to the trunk became the upper end of the bow. His personal weapon was about fifty inches long, and according to Theodora Kroeber, he made his bows three to four fingers wide at each side of the grip, which was slightly narrowed, depending upon whether he wanted a very powerful bow or a lighter one.[8] He backed his bows with deer leg sinew, and for some he made at the museum of the University of California he used Le Page's glue! He measured bows much as the Sioux did, and so made different lengths for different people. One in the museum at Berkeley must be fifty-five or fifty-six inches long, and others are shorter than his own of fifty inches. All his bows still in storage at the University Museum are beautifully made, but when I saw them, had been poorly cared for. It hurt to see them standing up in an old barrel in a corner of the basement. One had been broken in the usual way of museum bows, by stringing it backward. I was impressed that these bows were not nearly as wide as most California bows we see. In fact, the widest would not be over three fingers in width, and small fingers at that.

We knew Dr. Chamberlain, who had helped care for Ishi in his last illness. He said Ishi was the most intelligent man he ever met, bar none. That such a "primitive" man could make so great an adaptation to our modern "civilization" in so short a time is truly remarkable. Dr. Chamberlain told us that he made a death mask of Ishi but felt it did not do him justice. He wanted to remember him as he was when alive; so he destroyed the mask.

The Panamint Indians of Death Valley made bows about three feet long from desert juniper, preferring seasoned wood from a standing dead tree. They covered the sinew back with a rattlesnake skin. Snake skin was often used on bows of northeastern California also.

Most of the coastal California bows were sinew-backed and all were beautifully painted. The designs were the finest and most elaborate found anywhere. Representative collections of these bows are found in the California State Museum at Sacramento, the Field Museum in Chicago, The National Museum in Washington, D.C., and the Museum of the American Indian and the American Museum of Natural History in New York.

The glue for at least some of them was made "by boiling the gland of the lower jaw and the nose of the sturgeon."[9] The backs were whitened with clay just after the application of the wet sinew, then were painted when dry, usually in black and red, but sometimes using green also. Even plain wood bows with no sinew were nicely painted, sometimes on the back, sometimes on the belly, occasionally on both, again usually in red and black. Even some inland bows

Ishi, last of the Yahi. Courtesy of Lowie Museum of Anthropology, University of California.

and bows to the north, like those of the Modocs, were painted in similar fashion.

Bows of the Indians at the mouth of the Columbia River were like those farther south in California—short, wide, with sinew backs. On Vancouver Island bows were made of yew and crab apple, about three and a half feet long and two inches wide, with nicely recurved limbs. Farther up the coast, in the Northwest Coast area, some of the bows continued to be of California style, wide and flat, but somewhat longer. Cedar, some yew, and even birch and spruce were used. Maple, beech, and sometimes willow were used inland. Some of the bows of this region again were made like the Eskimo bows, with twisted sinew cording for backs instead of sinew laid in glue. They probably never could get it warm enough to use glue efficiently. The sinew cords were tightened by the use of two little ivory levers before using the bow and were relaxed again after use. Arrows were made of long splinters split from pine and spruce.

Thompson River Indians, who are of Salish stock, made little thirty-inch bows of cherry, about an inch and a half wide, sometimes covered with rattle-snake skin. One such little fellow in the Peabody Museum at Harvard University has small nocks with short buckskin fringe below them, and both the tips and handle are decorated with flicker feathers. They used serviceberry shoots for arrows and a quiver of wolverine skin.

Not far away, also in British Columbia, the Shuswaps make a small bow of juniper, or sometimes yew, with rattlesnake-skin and serviceberry arrows. In the same province the Sekanis use mountain maple, with sinew glued to the back with sturgeon glue and wrapped with sinew, for bows as much as 5 1/2 feet long. A little to the west, Carriers made their bows 4 feet long or some-times a trifle longer, also with glued sinew backs. Up on the Yukon, the Kutchins made a willow bow about 4 1/2 feet long, with a little stick about 3 inches long and 1 1/2 inches wide fastened perpendicularly to the bow just above the handle to catch the string so that it would not slap the hand or wrist in shooting. These bows were barely braced, being left almost straight so as not to have to bend the wood any farther than necessary. Willow is a supple wood when green, but when dry it bends only slightly without breaking.

Up in the true Eskimo country any kind of wood is at a premium. By mak-ing special trips to more forested regions the Eskimos sometimes obtained birch and willow, but generally they used driftwood, timber from wrecked ships, and sometimes reindeer antler. The antler bows were short, only about three feet long, spliced at the handle, and corded on the back with sinew like wooden bows. The wooden bows, however, were much longer, anywhere from about 54 to 62 inches in length, depending upon the locality. There are considerable differences in bows of the southern and northern Eskimos. I have an Eskimo bow of birch 54 1/2 inches long. It is triangular in cross section, flat on the back. It is perhaps forty-five or fifty years old and seems to have had a sinew-corded backing at one time. Since bows are seldom used any more, someone may have needed the sinew for some other purpose and removed it.

Some of the Eskimo bows have long ears, each one as much as a quarter as long as the entire bow. Some of these ears have a slight curve towards the string, just the opposite of the usual recurve. These ears have been criticized as being nonfunctional, but I do not agree. Perhaps they would not be as efficient as the usual recurve, but they would nevertheless add leverage to the limbs and increase both power and cast. The Eskimos are very practical people, and I cannot imagine they would go to all the trouble of making such ears if they served no purpose. I think they acted somewhat in the same capacity as the "working recurve" on modern bows.

Eskimo-type bows are also found in Siberia, and it would be interesting to know if the type was developed there or on this side of the water.

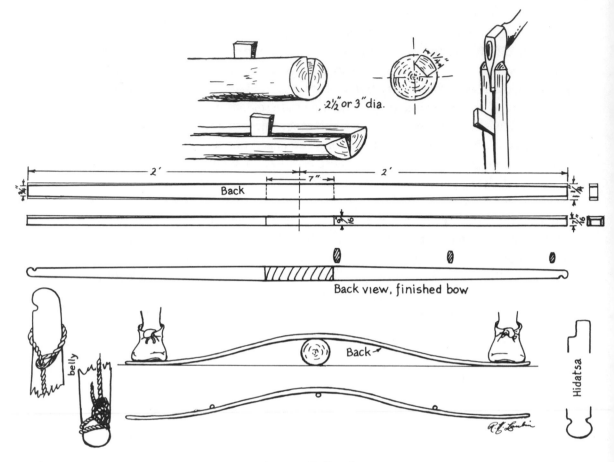

2½" or 3" dia.

2'

Back

7"

Back view, finished bow

belly

Back

Hidatsa

Making an Indian bow.

*Right,* Reginald Laubin (Tatanka Wanjila) demonstrating the Indian manner of carrying the shield and quiver.

*Below right,* Reginald Laubin (Tatanka Wanjila) demonstrating the position of the bow before drawing.

*Below,* shooting while wearing a shield and quiver. (This double-curved bow bends in the handle and kicks, but shoots hard.)

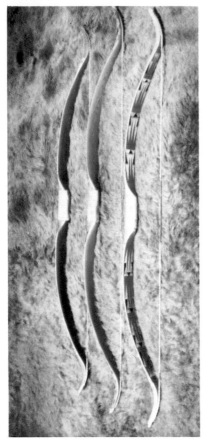

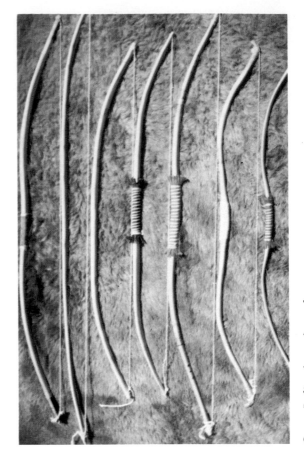

Same braced bows showing the bellies: *top,* Osage Orange; *center, yew; below,* yew with rawhide on the belly.

Same Indian bows braced.

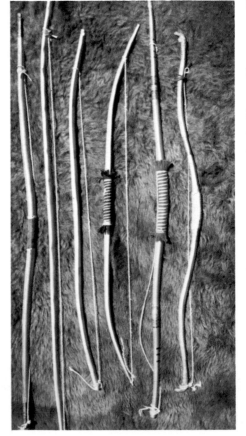

Three braced semi-Indian-style bows showing the backs: *top,* Osage Orange, Yurok design; *center,* yew with pine-snake skin; *below,* yew with rattlesnake skin.

Indian bows relaxed: *top to bottom,* Sioux sinew-backed bow, Cheyenne self bow, John Sitting Bull's Sioux self bow, Eagle Hawk's Sioux self bow, Laubin's Sioux sinew-backed bow, and Laubin's horn-and-sinew bow.

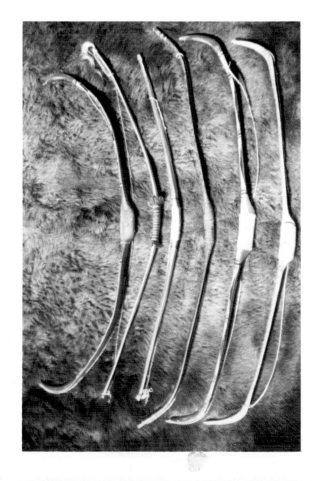

*Above left*, bow backs with California designs.

*Above right*, bow bellies with California designs.

*Left*, reflexed bows of various types relaxed.

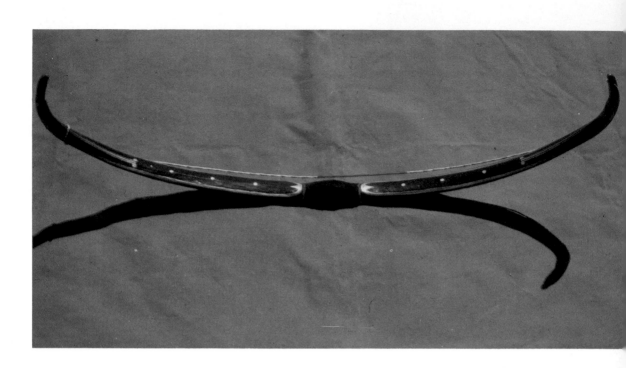

"Osage Turk" bow: *above,* back, relaxed; *below,* belly, braced, with Turkish-style arrow.

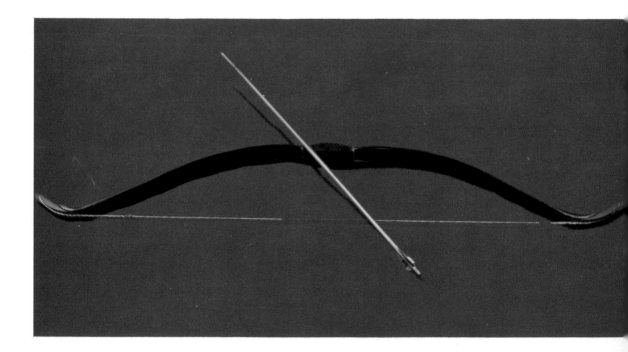

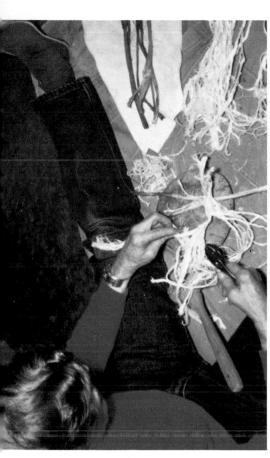

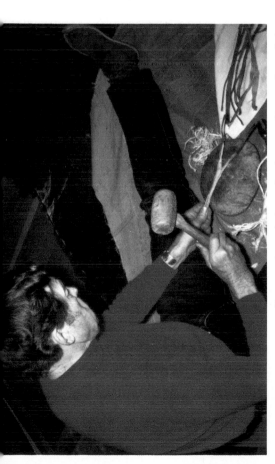

Preparation of sinew for bow making: *above left*, pounding; *above right*, shredding; *below left*, grading; *below right*, applying glue-soaked sinew to the bow back.

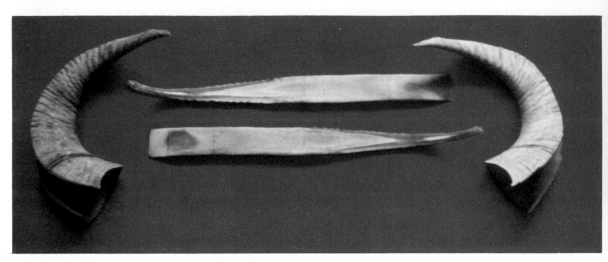

Two mountain-sheep horns after sawing off strips for bow limbs; and the two bow limbs after boiling, straightening, and rough shaping.

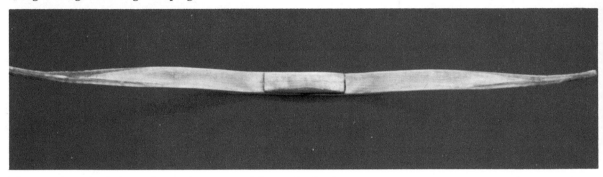

The two bow limbs joined together, viewed from the back.

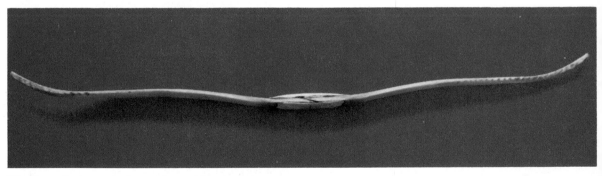

The bow limbs joined together, side view.

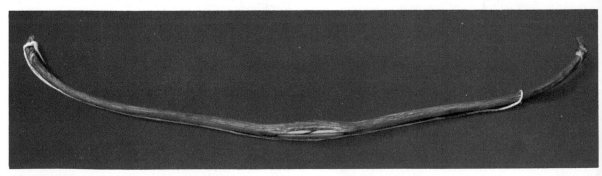

The mountain-sheep horn bow after the sinew had dried for two weeks, showing the increase in reflex.

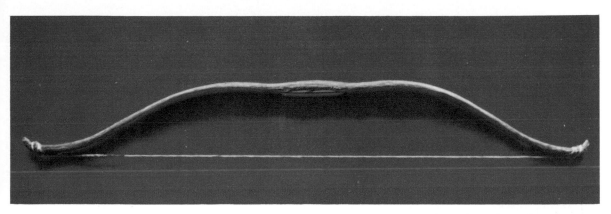

Mountain-sheep horn bow, first bracing.

Finished mountain-sheep horn bow, relaxed.

Finished mountain-sheep horn bow, braced.

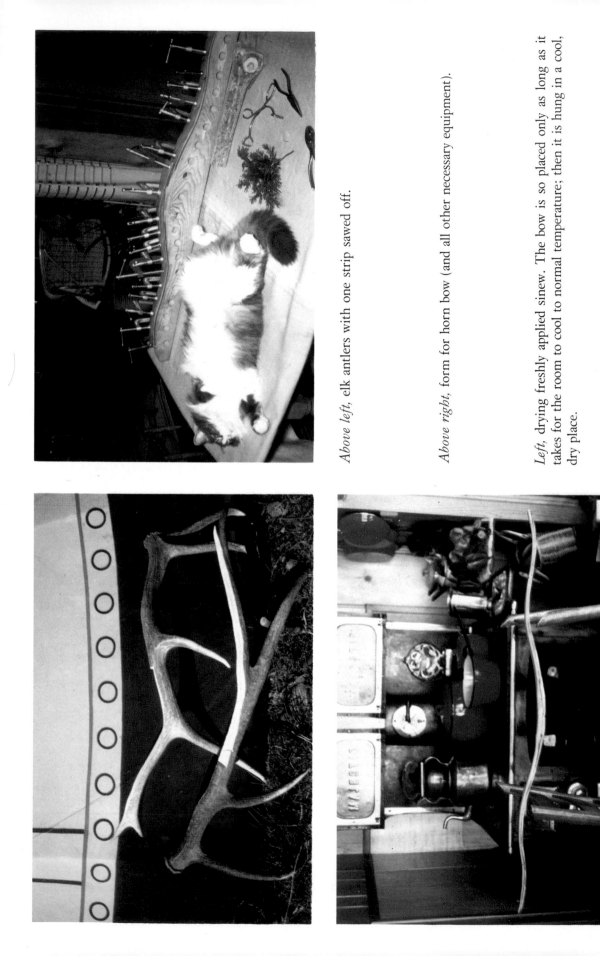

*Above left*, elk antlers with one strip sawed off.

*Above right*, form for horn bow (and all other necessary equipment).

*Left*, drying freshly applied sinew. The bow is so placed only as long as it takes for the room to cool to normal temperature; then it is hung in a cool, dry place.

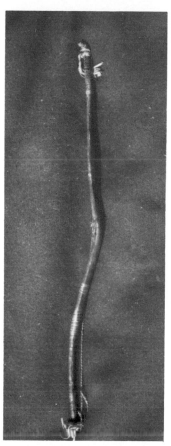

*Above left,* horn bow hanging to cure sinew.

*Above right,* Crow Indian mountain-sheep horn bow from the Vernon Collection, Colter Bay Museum, Grand Teton National Park.

*Left,* Laubin elk horn bow, braced.

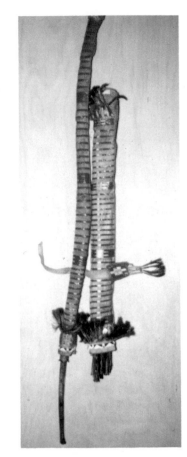

*Above left,* Sioux quiver of beaded buckskin, arrow cup, and bone-tipped arrows.

*Above right,* Cheyenne-style mountain-lion skin quiver, quilled and beaded.

*Right,* Sioux quilled quiver (with strap missing).

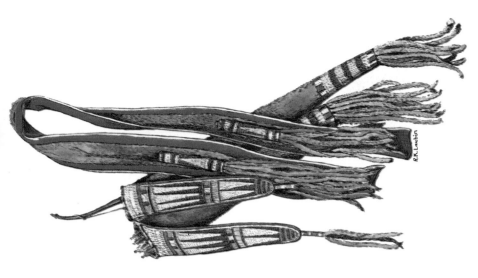

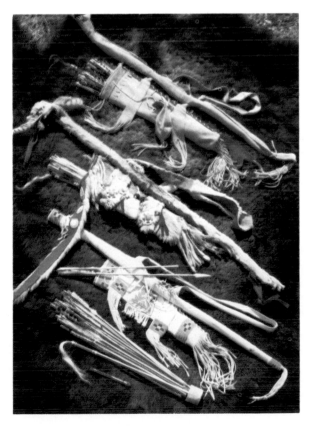

*Above left,* Apache-style quiver.

*Below left,* quivers: *left to right,* Sioux, Cheyenne, and Apache.

*Above right,* Crow otter-skin quiver from the Chandler Collection, Plains Indian Museum, Cody, Wyoming.

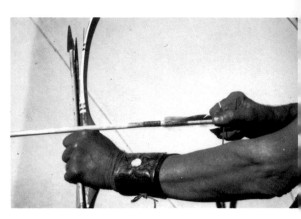

Primary arrow hold (outside view).

Primary arrow hold (inside view).

Secondary, or Cheyenne, arrow hold (outside view).

Secondary, or Cheyenne, arrow hold (inside view).

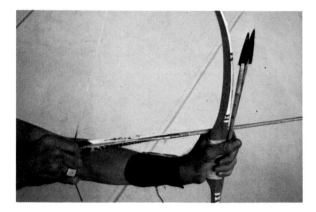

Tertiary, or Sioux, arrow hold (outside view).

Tertiary, or Sioux, arrow hold (inside view).

Mediterranean arrow hold (outside view).

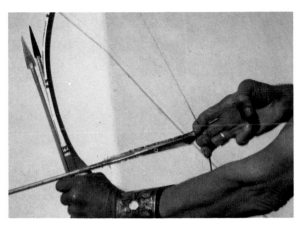

Mediterranean arrow hold (inside view).

Ishi's thumb hold (outside view).

Ishi's thumb hold (inside view).

Bracing, first method.

Bracing, second method.

Shooting a bow of the Martin type using the Mediterranean hold.

Thirty-two bows hanging from the authors' ceiling in Jackson's Hole, Wyoming.

Medicine Bow Society regalia.

Chief One Bull and Kills Pretty Enemy.

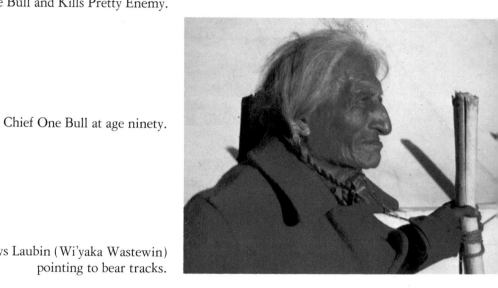

Chief One Bull at age ninety.

Gladys Laubin (Wi'yaka Wastewin)
pointing to bear tracks.

# 4

# Bow Making
# and Sinewed Bows

When I was a boy there was another youngster in the neighborhood who had
an outfit he called a "bonearra." I discovered that his bow was the "bonearra,"
and the arrow was the "bonearra stick." This was about the time I was getting
interested in "bosenarras" myself. My first bow was made of half of a barrel
hoop. Then I graduated to a bow made of umbrella staves tied together, and
later to one of green hickory which I laboriously cut with a not-too-sharp
jackknife on one of our hikes in the woods. Finally came the day when I got my
hands on some real archery information, and I have been fascinated by the
subject ever since.

I made my first longbow from a piece of white oak cut from a plank. I
had read that white oak would do for a bow, but it did not do too well. It broke
in a short time. My next try was from a white ash rake handle. This was easier
to get than a commercial bow stave; no one in our town had heard of an archery
shop. The rake handle soon became a longbow.

I made another bow sixty-five inches long from a slab of white ash picked
up from the discard pile at a sawmill. With it I earned my Boy Scout archery
merit badge under the old requirements of the 1920s. I was told that I was
the first in the state of Connecticut to receive it. Later the requirements were
considerably relaxed because they were too difficult and not enough boys were
getting the badge. I still have that old bow too.

Both of these ash bows followed the string so badly that they looked to be
strung all the time. However, they still shoot, after a fashion. I also have kept
an old six-foot lemonwood bow from this early period, apparently in perfect
shape, but it is so slow in comparison to the short, sinew-backed bows I have
used in recent years that I cannot imagine how I enjoyed it so much.

The first time I saw a bow with a sinew back I not only wanted to own one but wanted to be able to make one. However, by the time I went to live with the Indians all the old bow makers were gone. Although there were a few old warriors left, none of them knew all of the details of applying the sinew. Most of them had owned sinew-backed bows at one time or another, but, as mentioned earlier, making sinew-backed bows was almost a special trade, and not every man made them. All the reports I read of their construction were sketchy, but I eventually acquired enough information to make my first try.

For a time it looked as if the sinewed bow would come back into general use as several American archers began experimenting with sinew, and some of them had outstanding results. But the development of fiber-glass bows almost completely eliminated further interest in sinew. Very few of us are left who make sinewed bows. But those few are still convinced that they are the best. We have yet to see a fiber-glass bow that can outshoot or outlast a good sinew-backed bow. If the fiber glass is so good, why is even the most expensive bow guaranteed for only two years? I have sinewed bows I made twenty-five years ago that perform as well today as they did when they were made. In all that time I have broken only two bows, one that cracked on the belly when the string broke, and another that broke during bracing when allowed to twist out of control, again on the belly. Stringing the bow is the greatest hazard to long bow life. I have never had the sinew break or pull away, and I have never broken a bow during shooting. But, considering that it takes at least six months to finish a good sinew-backed bow, I realize it would be impossible to meet commercial demands, and few would be interested enough or able to afford to buy one.

When old-timers at Standing Rock told me my five-foot bow was too long, I decided to find out how a shorter one would behave. I have settled on bows between forty-five and fifty inches and have been very happy with them. However, I doubt they would be serviceable without being backed with sinew. Otherwise, I do not think even a fifty-inch bow would last very long if used continually. I feel that as a guarantee against breakage they must be sinew-backed.

Archers trying short bows have complained about finger pinch, which occurs when the string at full draw is at such an angle that it actually pinches the fingers and makes the release difficult. Of course, they insist on using twenty-six- or even twenty-eight-inch arrows, which naturally increases the difficulty. To eliminate this finger pinch, short fiber-glass bows are now being made deflexed, which to me implies about the same thing as following the

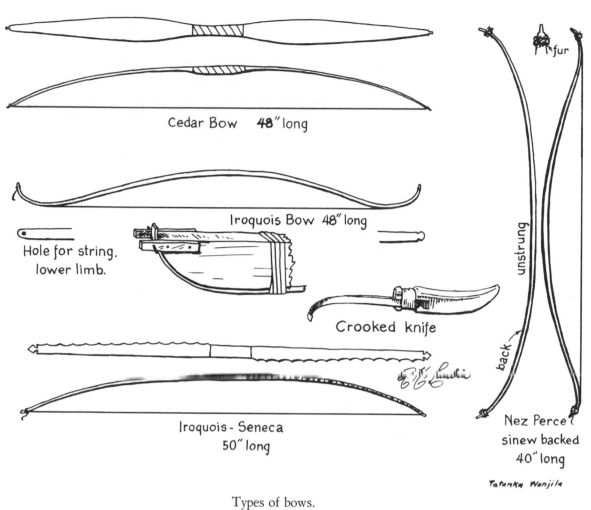

Cedar Bow   48" long

Iroquois Bow 48" long

Hole for string,
lower limb.

Crooked knife

Iroquois - Seneca
50" long

fur

unstrung

back

Nez Perce
sinew backed
40" long

Tatanka Wanjila

Types of bows.

string. They compensate somewhat for this by making the limbs with a working recurve, but to deliberately follow the string does not seem to me to be the best use of materials, when the effort all through the years has been to eliminate string follow. This deflexing, combined with stringing the bow very high, does eliminate finger pinch because the bow is half drawn before the arrow is placed on the string. But it would seem to me to be much simpler and more satisfactory merely to make the bow as it should be made, preferably reflexed because this gives the most power and snappiest cast, and to use a shorter arrow. Taking the Sioux average arrow length of twenty-three inches as my standard I have had such good results that I have used it ever since.

If a satisfactory score is the only objective, I can see that even modern plastic and glass archery has some inducement as a sport over firearms because I think it takes more skill to make a good archery score, no matter what kind of tackle is used, than to make a good score with firearms. There is some thrill in being able to handle a powerful bow efficiently because the force of the arrow as well as the direction of its flight depend upon the archer. A novice pulling the trigger on a rifle with the greatest muzzle velocity and farthest range can shoot the bullet just as far and just as hard as a seasoned veteran. Shooting with firearms is entirely a test of skill. Archery tests both skill and strength, and also craftsmanship in those who make their own tackle.

How much more thrilling it is not only to command this power but to create the weapon that utilizes it! This is why archery is for me the perfect sport and hobby. Modern archery can be as expensive as any sport, but a person can still make, from native materials and with few tools, weapons that are both efficient and satisfying to the craftsman. To me nothing compares with making my own equipment and then seeing it in action. No matter how good a bow I could buy, nor what kind of results I might obtain with it, it could never give me the pleasure I get from making really good tackle myself.

My first attempts, barring English longbows, were with the shorter, wide, and flat bows that were popular just before glass bows came on the scene. Except for a much heavier handle and greater length, they were like Indian bows. I have made duplicates of several Indian bows as well.

Many Indian bows were made from small trees 2 1/2 to 3 inches in diameter, which, if carefully split down the center, might yield two bows. Some were even cut from heavy saplings, about 1 1/2 inches in diameter, which usually would furnish only one bow because one side was whittled away rather than split. The splitting of such a small sapling would seldom be accurate enough to result in two staves. Bows made from such material were usually half round in cross section, whereas staves split from heavier wood could be made into bows with rectangular cross sections.

It has already been brought out that many tribes preferred seasoned wood from standing trees, which had been killed by lightning or which, in the desert, had died recently enough that the wood was seasoned rather than deteriorated.

M. R. Harrington[1] tells of a Leni Lenape (Delaware) method of obtaining

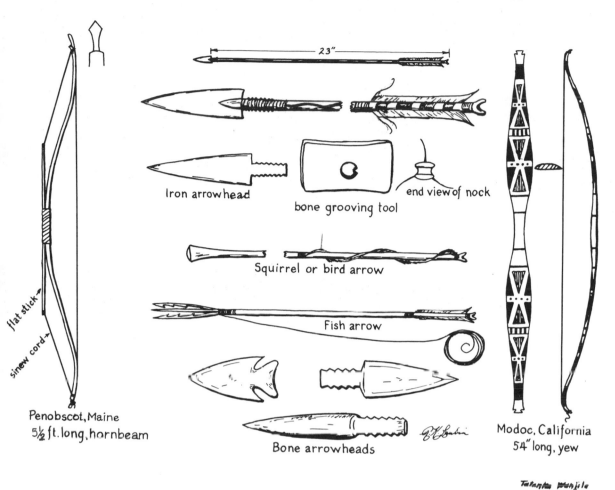

Penobscot, Maine
5½ ft. long, hornbeam

Iron arrowhead

bone grooving tool

end view of nock

Squirrel or bird arrow

Fish arrow

Bone arrowheads

Modoc, California
54" long, yew

More bow types, arrows, and points.

a bow stave. The bow maker selected a hickory tree of about three spans
around, then made an offering of tobacco and a prayer to the tree for the use
of its wood and that the bow might be a good one that would send its arrows
straight and true. He then sawed a cut about an inch deep a foot above the
base of the tree, sawed another cut about five feet above the first, then cut
parallel lines up the trunk connecting these cuts, and split off the stave thus
outlined, using wedges made of antler.

All the tools that are really needed to manufacture a bow from the stave are a good, sharp hand ax, a jackknife, a couple of files—a half-round wood file and a small round file—and sandpaper ranging from coarse to fine. A small vise helps, and to make a joined bow a very sharp, fine saw is necessary. Better yet, access to a band saw is the easiest way to make an accurate fishtail splice. A good scraper is also a big asset. The best can be made from an old file about 1 1/2 inches in width, ground on the edges to a concave surface using a fine grinding wheel. However, even pieces of glass can make good scrapers. Indians used mussel shells and stone scrapers, and glass after it became available. I use a hand ax for all my roughing out. If you cut your own wood, some wedges are needed to help split it into staves.

Eastern Indians made almost the entire bow using a crooked knife, which was their all-around tool. The original was made from a beaver's tooth. Later ones were made from old files, drawing the temper with heat, grinding them to a sharp edge, then shaping them to the desired curve or hook on the end, and retempering them.

Several bow woods have already been mentioned. Before Indians had steel tools they made their bows from green wood and seasoned them after they were made, greasing them well to prevent splitting and warping. But it is still better to use seasoned wood in the first place. Eventually, to behave well and to last well, the bow must be seasoned, and there is no short cut. The only wood I know of that will make a reasonably good bow while still green is red cedar. But red cedar makes a delicate bow, whether green or dry. Good bow wood should be seasoned at least a year. One of my best bows is made of Osage orange cut more than fifty years ago, but I have also made good bows of wood seasoned only one or two years.

I have made several wide thin bows similar to coastal California bows, from 2 to 2 1/2 inches in width but only about 1/4 inch thick. They shoot beautifully, but in theory at least, a narrower, thicker bow should shoot farther because the more resistance the bow builds up as it is drawn the more cast it will have when it is released. Also, with an all-wood bow there is less danger of breakage in the wide thin type, but with a sinew-back there is little likelihood of either kind breaking.

For practical reasons, because soft woods are usually more brittle than hard woods, Indians who used the soft ones made wide thin bows, and Indians who had access to hard woods made narrower but thicker ones. Yew would be an exception as a brittle soft wood, but Indians who used it usually wanted very short bows; so again the wide bow gave better service.

It seems strange that the two very best bow woods, Oregon yew and Osage orange, are almost exact opposites in some respects. The yew is light in weight and quite soft. The Osage is very heavy and quite hard. Both are somewhat difficult to work because of twists in the grain and because there are often knots to contend with.

When the wood is seasoned, even if some cracks have developed one can usually work around them without much difficulty. Even if a stave is lost in splitting the log, one has not lost all the work necessary to make a bow. The log should be seasoned with the bark on to help prevent splitting and checking, and it is a good idea to paint or varnish the ends. It should be left in a dry place at normal temperature.

My bows are primarily of Osage orange,* although I have made several of yew that shoot beautifully. Yew is much easier to work, but I am always a little leery of using it in cold weather. I have also used ash and hickory and have found that they make good bows when sinew-backed; the sinew eliminates their biggest faults, string follow and sluggishness. I have tried many designs, but believe the one developed by the late Robert Martin of Wisconsin, a famous bowyer well-acquainted with Indians of his area, to be the best. It incorporates ears about 5 1/2 inches long which are very narrow when viewed from the back or belly of the bow but are quite thick when viewed from the side. This design gives the necessary whip action at the end of the shot for the most efficient flight of the arrow and eliminates extra weight that could cause sluggish and jarring performance. Being heavier on the side prevents the ear shearing off and produces stability. To make a bow of this design requires much practice and skill and should not be attempted as a first trial. It would be better first to try a simple Indian style like some of the ones illustrated.

Most of my bows of Martin design are made of two pieces because this makes it possible to give them quite a set back—as much as three inches in a four-foot bow. I will not go into detail about making the splice at the handle; that has been illustrated in a number of archery books. A little trick I have discovered to get the ears to line up correctly is to bend them before I join

---

*The name Osage orange was given to this wood because it was first reported in use by the Osage Indians of Missouri and Arkansas and because of its color, which ranges from pale yellow or orange to deep brown. It belongs to the mulberry family. The wood was prized by many tribes and bow staves made of it were popular articles of intertribal trade. French traders dubbed the wood *"bois d'arc"* (wood for the bow), which was corrupted by American traders to "bow dark." It was sometimes called "mock orange," because its fruit resembles a very rough, green orange, and was sometimes called "hedge apple" because of this inedible fruit and because it was early introduced into areas not in its original range for use as hedge material before the development of barbed wire.

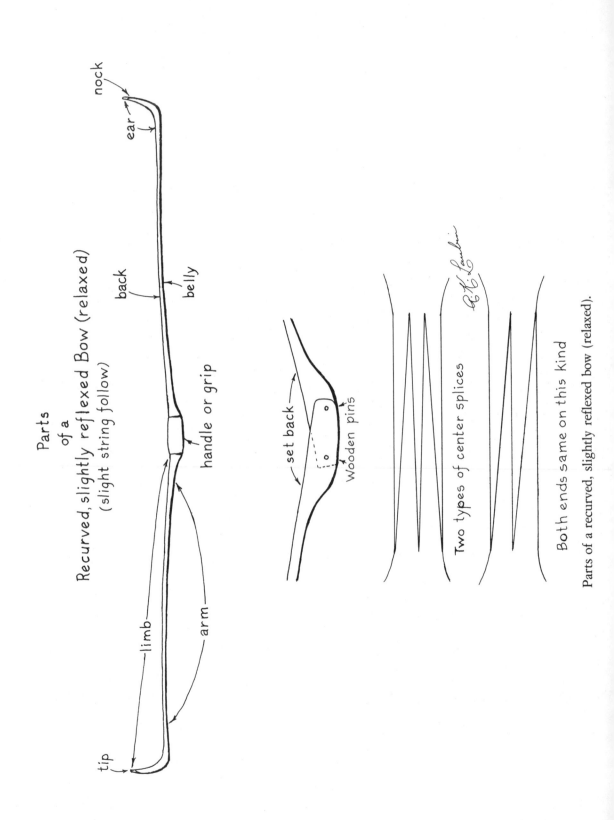

Parts
of a
Recurved, slightly reflexed Bow (relaxed)
(slight string follow)

nock

ear

back

belly

handle or grip

limb

arm

tip

set back

Wooden pins

Two types of center splices

Both ends same on this kind

Parts of a recurved, slightly reflexed bow (relaxed).

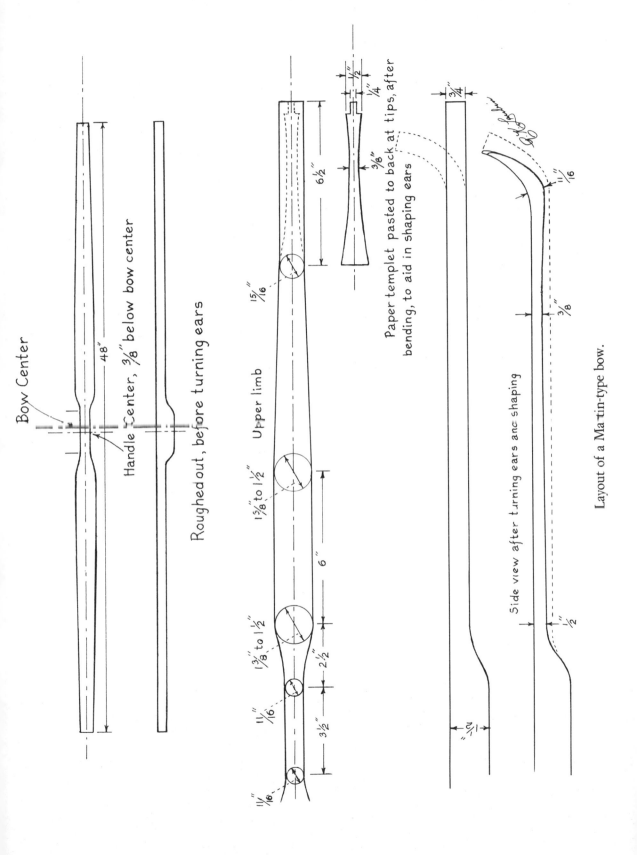

Bow Center

48"

Handle Center, 3/8" below bow center

Roughed out, before turning ears

Upper limb

15/16"

1 3/8 to 1 1/2"

6"

1 3/8 to 1 1/2"

2 1/2

11/16"

3 1/2

11/16"

1/2"

1/4"

6 1/2"

3/8"

Paper templet pasted to back at tips, after bending, to aid in shaping ears

3/4"

11/16"

3/8"

1/2

Side view after turning ears and shaping

1 1/2"

Layout of a Martin-type bow.

the two halves. This way I can lay out and saw the splice after the ears are turned and line them up perfectly. Even when this method is used, there are times, due to peculiarities in the wood, when a bow will go out of line after it is made. It is then necessary to heat the limbs and twist the ears to change the alignment and bring the bow back to true. Usually, though, the ears hold true and no such trouble is experienced. Forms for turning the ears can be made of two-by-fours that have been shaped to the curve desired. The wood should be heated in a steam box, or boiled, to soften it before bending. Boiling is the easiest and requires the least equipment, but it takes 3 1/2 to 4 hours of boiling to soften it sufficiently. By using two pieces for the bow, both ends can be boiled at once, saving much time, although saving time was not particularly important to Indians. A big, heavy coffee pot does the job nicely.

The main reason some people consider highly reflexed and recurved bows to be unstable is that they are not well made in the first place. They may be out of balance or out of line, or both. The making of such bows is an art that takes a long time to learn; so it is little wonder that there are few left who want to devote the necessary time to it when good bows are now produced in factories using more or less assembly-line procedures.

If efficiency, target scores, saving time, and other considerations are of utmost importance, then the modern bows will suffice; but for anyone with a desire to express himself as a craftsman who likes to work simply with limited equipment there is no greater satisfaction than learning to build bows that equal any of the machine-made products in performance. For those of us who still do like to make our own equipment the challenge is greater than ever because one cannot even buy wooden staves from the archery suppliers nowadays. Procuring the necessary materials is still a project in itself, as it was years ago when archery made its first entree as a recognized sport.

The first time I put sinew on a bow I did so mostly by guesswork. I had some very long sinew, probably horse, that my Indian mother, Scarlet Whirlwind, gave to me. In those days you could buy hide glue in almost any hardware store and I got grade-A hide glue. I thought this would be the nearest thing to the glue the Indians made from hide scrapings, hoofs, and sinew scraps. The sinew was from the loin, which lies in a wide thin band along the spine. Some reports give the impression that bows were backed by applying one of these bands to each end of the bow and joining them at the handle. Other accounts say the sinew was torn apart into fine threads. So, partly because "mother" had already used some of this sinew for thread and it was pretty well shredded, I finished shredding it into long pieces about an eighth of an inch wide or less.

I covered the flake glue (afterward I learned it could also be bought powdered or pulverized) with rain water, and when it had become like gelatin, placed the container (a tin can) in a pan of hot water and kept it as hot as my hand could bear until it all liquefied. I then poured this liquid glue into a bread pan and set it in a dishpan of hot water, which I kept comfortably hot on a gasoline camp stove. Later I discovered that a temperature between 120 and 125 degrees was ideal.

As an experiment, just to learn how good a glue the Indians could produce, I made some glue from elk dewclaws, hoofs, and sinew scraps. After boiling these for an hour or so and skimming off the residue which came to the surface, I continued simmering them for several hours until the resulting mass (mess) was about the consistency of the hide glue I had been using. This I poured into a shallow granite pan to dry. As it dried it pulled the granite coating right off of the pan! Although I did not make enough of this glue to use for sinewing a bow, I did try it on other things, and I am sure it would have worked out as well as the commercial hide glue. I was convinced that the Indians knew how to make really good glue.

One thing I want to make clear. A recent book states that the Indians *boiled* the sinew before applying it to the bow. The author must have obtained his information from an earlier writer who made the same mistake. Neither could know anything about sinew to make such a statement. You can make *glue* from sinew by boiling it for a long time as both Turks and Indians did, but if you so much as dip the sinew in boiling water you will ruin it for bow backing or for any purpose other than glue. It will shrivel out of shape, and you cannot bring it back, no matter how hard you try. The glue itself should never be so hot that it is uncomfortable to the fingers when immersing the sinew.

I soaked the sinew strips, or threads, in water for an hour or more until they became completely soft because all the sinew I had seen the Indians use had been soaked first. Indian women when sewing wet the threads in their mouths. I spread the sinews out on towels to absorb the excess water, then took each individual strand, dipped it in the hot glue, worked it through my fingers, and laid it on the bow. The modern epoxy and resin glues will not work on sinew and rawhide. I have tried them!

Some descriptions state that the sinew was started at the bow handle and worked out to the tips, but it seemed to me to lay on better if I started at the tips and worked back toward the handle. All the Indian bows that I had seen had some sinew lapped completely over the end of the bow and around onto the belly for an inch or so. So I started the sinew at the tip with enough to turn a couple of inches under on the belly and brought it back towards the handle.

The strips were not quite long enough to reach the handle; so I filled in with shorter pieces, staggering them in order that all the joinings would not come in one line across the bow. Later I came across an account of Indians laying on the sinew beginning at the ends and working towards the center; so I felt I was doing all right. Accounts of recent bowyers using sinew, as well as stories about Turkish bowyers, state that the sinew was laid on beginning at the center and working out to the tips. Nevertheless, I had such good results doing it my way that I have continued that way ever since, and if I do say so, I have never seen any sinew job on a bow that looks better or smoother than mine.

Some Indian bows were quite thinly lined with sinew on the back, rather than truly sinew-backed. The primary purpose in such cases was to prevent breakage. The sinew also restricted string follow, although it did not completely eliminate it, and even such a thin layer added considerably to the strength of the bow. Anyone who says that sinew adds nothing to the strength or cast of a bow has had no experience with sinew.

This first sinewing operation, although admittedly a messy and sticky one, was so fascinating and turned out so well that I have been making sinewed bows ever since. This first experience taught me two things I had not planned on nor thought of. I allowed the bow to dry a couple of weeks, and in that time the bow, which I had previously shot a few times at about half draw just to test its tiller and to make comparisons later, (1) took a slight reflex and (2) became much stronger even though it had followed the string considerably beforehand. A year later, after much shooting, the reflex had increased rather than decreased. At first I was so worried that I would leave the bow strung, sometimes for several days, but after unstringing it would come back to a slightly reflexed position and in a day or so more would be back to its highest reflex.

This convinced me that sinew was really a marvelous material, and I still think no glass or plastic can compare with it. I have used sinew from deer, buffalo, elk, moose, and cow. Although this first bow was backed with horse loin sinew, and I have made a couple of other bows of deer loin sinew, I began to use leg sinew, which is far easier to obtain. Most hunters throw the legs away, but none of them know how to remove the loin sinew,[2] and they destroy it with their white man's way of butchering.

For bow making the leg sinew is as good or better than loin, even though it is shorter and is considerably more difficult to prepare. I generally use elk because it is easiest to get here around Jackson's Hole. All sinew, once dried and shredded, looks and handles alike, but I feel sure the elk is superior in some ways to the cattle. At least, elk sinew will draw the wood up more than an equal amount of cattle sinew, giving the bow more reflex. However, it also seems to have more of a tendency to cause longitudinal cracks on the belly because of its extra tension. Fortunately these cracks are usually fine and do no actual harm.

I have made several bows of Osage orange, each with a thin layer of sapwood left on, and I find that with a heavy layer of sinew there are fewer, or no belly cracks. They shoot just as hard and fast as the bows that are all heartwood. In comparing self bows of Osage orange, perhaps the all-heartwood bow will outperform one with a sapwood back, although I am not entirely convinced of this. I am certain that if the bows are backed with sinew there is no appreciable difference.

After I had been making sinewed bows for several years, I found out that it is unnecessary to wash or degrease the sinew, or even to soak it. I have seen no difference in the results, and it does save a certain amount of work. When the sinew is pounded thoroughly — I use a heavy mallet on a granite boulder — the outer skin, which may be greasy and dirty, peels off and the underlaying sinew is never greasy. It is a lot of work to hammer and pull a leg tendon to pieces, and four to six tendons are needed, depending upon whether they are from hind or forelegs. But eventually it gets done. I pull them apart so thoroughly that the tiny threads look like shoemaker's linen; then I sort them for length and gather them into small bundles, a dozen threads to a bundle.

I still prepare the glue as described before, but now usually set it on an electric burner at "simmer," which keeps the right temperature. I also heat the room in which I work to eighty five or ninety degrees. I did not do this for my earlier bows; I just took the temperature of the room as it was. I even sinewed one bow in the basement of the park superintendent's house, and it came out very well. That was more than twenty years ago, and the bow is still in fine shape. However, a hot room does help because the glue tends not to jell as quickly, and you can take your time without feeling rushed.

First, I scrape the back of the bow with a hack saw blade, then I go over the bow with a 10 percent lye solution, let it dry, then rinse it off thoroughly with boiling water. A detergent or naphtha soap can be used, but the lye is better, at least for Osage orange. The scratches from the saw blade give a rough surface to which the glue can adhere. The back of the bow *is not cut* as one recent writer declared, but merely scratched and roughened a bit to help the glue adhere. Next I give the entire bow, back and belly, a couple of coats of sizing, which is the same glue diluted about two to one with rain water. When the sizing has dried, I gently warm the bow over the heater and then begin the actual sinewing.

Each little bundle of dry sinew is thoroughly immersed in the warm, not-too-thick glue, swished around in it, and pulled through the fingers from the center outward to each end, before laying it on. For an average bow I use about eight bunches on each limb for a first course, mainly down the center, and add a second course immediately over the first, this time going well over the sides, using about twelve bunches.

Some California Indians are reported to have bound the sinew with bark after it was applied, but it is not necessary to wrap the sinew if you apply it well and have the glue at the right consistency. The California Indians hung their bows in the sweat house to cure, where it was quite damp. The bows would thus cure very slowly, but it may have been necessary to wrap them during the process because of the dampness.

I have tried laying on one course, letting it dry a couple of weeks, then adding a second course and letting it dry for six months in the basement where it is cool and dry. I have seen no difference in results when applying both courses, one right after the other, and letting the bow dry only twelve days to two weeks. With both methods I often have had trouble with fine line cracks on the belly when using the amount of sinew I like to hold a good reflex. If anything, the longer cure seems worse. It seems to work out a little better if I begin shooting the bow within a couple of weeks. But you still may not know just what the bow will do for at least six months, and it takes a couple of years to bring the sinew to its final cure. After all, an old Turkish bowyer would not let a bow out of his shop for at least five years!

A couple of bows line-cracked so badly that I faced the belly with thin deer rawhide. Rawhide should be applied wet and with the glue on the outer, or hair, side, which, of course, is then turned to the wood so that the flesh side is the outer surface. I use two strips of rawhide, each half the length of the bow; start each strip at the center of the handle and stretch it out to the tip as tightly as possible; tie it in place at each end; then carefully wrap it in place with a crisscross bandage like that described later for covering a bow back with snake skin. This is one case where you can use either casein or resin glue instead of hide glue, but they will not work for sinew. The rawhide hides the cracks, gives a beautiful surface on which to paint designs if you care to, and it is beautiful in its own right. As far as I can tell, it adds little or no strength to the bow, nor does it impede its performance in any way. I imagine it is something like adding a very thin strip of horn, for horn and hide are of about the same physical composition.

After learning how well the rawhide on the belly behaved, I made several bows on which I glued a strip of rawhide to the bellies *before* applying the sinew to the backs. The results so far have been 100 percent satisfactory. After the sinew cured for several weeks, I peeled and scraped off the rawhide and found no belly cracks. Perhaps a strip of tightly woven canvas, linen, or other fabric that will not stretch would work as well as the rawhide to prevent the belly cracks, but on the other hand, the rawhide applied wet will shrink as it dries and help deter the wood from cracking because the cracking is caused by the tension of the sinew drying on the opposite side of the wood. However, the no-stretch fabric might be worth a try, to save the trouble and expense of preparing the rawhide, which must be discarded after the sinew has cured. As I see it, there are three choices: take a chance that the wood will not crack; if it does, add rawhide to cover the cracks and as a final finish to the belly; or glue a strip of rawhide or other no-stretch material to the belly before sinewing and remove it after the sinew has cured.

The ancient Egyptians sometimes applied a thin layer of sinew to the belly of a bow and a heavy layer to the back. I tried this, and it worked out very well, but I could not get used to the appearance of sinew on the belly.

Tillering the bow is probably the most important part of the entire manufacture. The final success of the bow depends upon it. Both limbs must be brought to the same perfect curve so that when strung the bow bends the same in each limb. If the bow is one with a shorter lower limb, the distance from the string to the belly when braced will be from 1/4 to 3/8 inch less on the lower limb than on the upper. If the limbs are of equal length, as on most Indian bows, then the string height must be the same on each limb. There must be no sharp places, no angles, anywhere—only beautiful, smooth curves, both in the braced position and at full draw.

Tillering is usually a long, tedious job requiring patience and a good eye, but the final results are worth the effort. It cannot be done in a hurry—only a little at a time with a rasp or scraper, testing often, with no seesawing (that is, taking off more than is necessary on one limb, then having to take more off the other limb to bring the bow back to balance). This is like needing more butter to go with the bread, then more bread to go with the butter. You can end up with a bow that pulls about fifteen pounds!

If the bow is tillered at about half draw before sinewing, I have learned to apply the sinew so evenly that I seldom have to retiller the bow, unless it comes out so strong I cannot manage it; then I have to work down both limbs and thus must tiller the wood again. Of course, if you put sinew on a well-tillered bow, and it is out of balance when the sinew has set, it naturally means the sinew is at fault and that some of it must be removed with a file. But, as I say, I seldom have to touch the sinew, and it is so pretty untouched that it adds extra attractiveness to the bow's appearance.

Many Indians added a snake skin over the sinew, which not only gave the bow a mighty businesslike appearance but also was some protection for the sinew against moisture and against fraying. If you do have to file the sinew to balance the bow, no matter how careful you are it may eventually raise up a fiber here and there. This is another reason I do not like to touch the sinew if I can help it. In this case the snake skin is a happy addition.

When I do not use a snake skin, I usually paint the sinew with a California Indian design, which is also very attractive. I have used rattlesnake, black-snake, and pine-snake skins. Any snake skin can be used, if long enough. If not, two can be used joined at the center and covered at the joining with a leather or thong-wrapped handle. The snake skins should be thoroughly scraped and cleaned, and any loose scales removed. This is a smelly, repulsive operation. Although not really necessary, it may be a good idea to soak the skins in a salt and sulphuric-acid solution, being sure to neutralize them afterward in a solution of baking soda. The skin is applied to the bow wet, with the same hot hide glue used for sinewing. The sinew back should first be sized with a thinner solution of glue. For convenience the skin is first rolled up, the glue is applied to the sinew back, and the skin unrolled into position. It should then be wrapped with a two-inch bandage, being careful not to pull the skin to one side. After drying a couple of days the bandage is removed, and the skin trimmed to fit the bow, flush with the edge of the belly.

The snake skin should be laid on so that the head end is at the top of the bow. The rattlesnake has a pretty black-banded end on his skin just before the rattles. In historical accounts it is mentioned that sometimes the rattle was even left on as further ornament.

I remember hearing years ago that Indians sometimes covered a bow with intestine instead of snake skin. I have done this a couple of times. The entire bow could be encased in intestine, but I merely wanted it on the back and so split the intestine up one side and glued it on. Indians may have used intestine for the same reasons they used snake skin—to help keep out dampness or to prevent the sinew from fraying, although the latter is an almost unknown risk if the sinew is properly applied and does not have to be scraped or filed to balance the bow.

I had some seal intestine given to me by a friend who traveled to Alaska, and some other from a steer, which I got from a packing house. I told them I wanted the large intestine, and they really gave it to me large—about fifty feet of the stuff! It was already wrapped when I arrived, and I did not want to seem unappreciative by unwrapping it, so I took the whole caboodle.

Later I cut off the few feet I needed for a couple of bows, but what a job it was to get rid of the rest of it! We did not want to leave it just any old place, so decided to take it to a dump. When we arrived there was a big sign, "$200 Fine for Disposing of Any Animal Remains." At the next town we saw a big packing plant, so headed for it. I told the manager about our dilemma, and although I am certain he thought I was slightly demented, he told me to throw it on their own refuse truck, which I did with a great sigh of relief.

The intestine worked out beautifully. After slitting the intestine, washing and rinsing it thoroughly, I applied it just as I had the snake skin. When dried on the bow it was so thin and smooth that it was almost invisible. To save the intestine not used at this time I dried it by hanging it over a pole. It shrank up so much it looked like a brown string, but it will swell up on soaking to its original size and will stretch almost unbelievably in width.

The bows I have been making on Martin's design actually incorporate the principles that have been discovered by Indians of different parts of the country. In the East bows were often nicely recurved at the ends but seldom if ever reflexed at the center. Most Plains bows were reflexed and double-curved. Some California bows had not only a high reflex but also slightly recurved tips, which may have helped some but were really not as efficient as they could have been. Martin's design gives the bow the best of both principles—the most from the recurves plus the advantage of the reflex. So these bows are really advanced Indian bows—short, smooth, and fast, with no kick and no stack, very light in the hand, and sweet to shoot.

Bows of the Martin type are from 1 3/8 inches to 1 1/2 inches wide and 47 to 52 inches long, with limbs 1/2 inch thick at the thickest part where they swell near the handle, which is only 7/8 inch wide, and 3/8 inch at their thinnest. The ears are 21/32 inch thick and 3/8 inch wide. The handle is 3 1/2 inches long, and I usually make mine about 1 1/4 inches thick, although it can be made as heavy as wanted. The thicknesses given are before the sinew is applied. They vary, of course, upon tillering to desired strength.

I have made bows of this style drawing from thirty-five to seventy-five pounds. Acquaintances with similar bows have put 22-inch arrows, with Indian-style fletching and points 2 1/2 inches long of razor-blade steel, completely through deer, with the arrow falling to the ground on the other side, and they have entirely pierced black bear. So there is no doubt of the efficiency of these little bows.

When I paint a bow I sometimes paint the back, sometimes the belly, occasionally both. I use casein tempera paints because they look the most like original Indian paints, and they are practically waterproof. If painting the back I coat the sinew first with a white base, then lay on the designs in black and red. When painting the belly I use the natural background as a base, whether it is wood or rawhide. After painting I give the bow a coat of dull-finish varnish and every so often rub the bow lightly with a mixture of cedar and boiled-linseed oil—I use this in place of the bear grease, deer brains, or deer fat used by the Indians, although on the real Indian-type bows I have made I have used bear grease.

I usually wrap the handle with a wide buckskin thong. Some bows from California and also some from the Plateau had a small band of fur below the nocks which deadened the twang of the bowstring and at the same time made an attractive decoration. Some fancy Plains bows, of either horn or wood, had a lock of dyed horsehair at one or both tips for added decoration.

Indians always kept material on hand for making new bows and arrows because, no matter how careful they were, bows broke and arrows were lost and it was essential that new ones be procured immediately. There was always at least one bow stave and one bundle of arrow materials hanging high in the lodge, where they would season well and be available whenever needed.

Indians took the best possible care of their archery tackle, frequently oiling or greasing the bow, straightening arrows, tightening the points by rewrapping the sinew, and making up new strings. For them the equipment was for survival as well as for sport and recreation.

Among all the tribes with which I am acquainted women were not permitted to handle a warrior's equipment, including bows and arrows. It was thought that such contamination could render them useless or inefficient, although through certain rituals and a ceremonial cleansing their power could be restored.

## OBSERVATIONS

After reconsidering many bows it seems that, in regard to line cracks on the belly, the amount of sinew is not as important as the thickness of the wood. Thin bows, whether narrow or wide, seldom crack, and when they do, do not crack as much, even when covered with half their thickness of sinew. Of course, a narrow thin bow is going to be a light bow. A thick wooden bow is apt to develop line cracks unless a fairly thin coat of sinew is used. Just how to explain this I do not know, but this is the way it works out.

The only way, then, of achieving a maximum of reflex in a wooden bow without belly cracks is to make it light, which must be an important reason why the Turks, Orientals, and eventually Plains and Plateau Indians came to use horn.

Generally bows containing both heart and sapwood crack the least. Yew has shown less tendency to crack than Osage orange, but sometimes chrysals, which can be worse. Even yew line-cracked, however, when a rather heavy layer of sinew was applied to a heavy bow of heartwood only. Gluing rawhide on the belly *before* sinewing, and removing it after six months seemed to prevent cracks on a couple of bows I made—one yew and one Osage.

Occasionally, even when the ears have been lined up perfectly at the time of sinewing the bow, and after drying for two or three weeks, when shooting the bow one or both ears will go out of line enough to throw off the string. At first I thought this was caused by the sinew on the ears; so I stopped putting sinew on them. I knew the Turks did not put sinew on the ears. But in this case it made no difference, so I decided that the ears twisted merely as a result of certain stresses in the wood itself and that these did not show up until the bow had seen some use.

The ears always twist towards the weaker side. Therefore, even if the surfaces of the bow look perfectly parallel, if the bow needs any reduction in weight or any further tillering it should be scraped down on the stronger side, even if (again due to peculiarities in the wood itself) this seems to be the thinner side.

If the bow needs no tillering, the ears can be lined up with heat, as mentioned earlier. If it is found that only one limb needs heat, the other should be heated anyway, even though its line does not need to be changed.

Regardless of the contour of the back, the longitudinal lines of the grain on the belly should be centered as much as possible—not running off to one side. In the case of a sinew-backed bow it is more important that the belly be right than the back. I have made several bows where I have had to cut through the grain on the back to some extent in order to have the grain come out right on the belly. If the sinew is properly applied, the bow will not break due to this tampering with the grain on the back.

Sometimes I have finished a bow with wax rather than with varnish or oil, but in this case the mixture of cedar and linseed oil can later be applied without ill effect on the wax.

It has long been pointed out that an archer should not be "over-bowed," but the reason usually given is that he must be able to draw the arrow to the head in order to aim properly. Even without this consideration of aiming, even if it were not necessary to aim, if he wanted only to make a long shot, he would find that a bow within his strength with which he could draw a proper arrow to the head would cast that arrow farther than if he used a much heavier bow but could draw it only part way. Apparently, no matter how strong a bow is, it cannot be used efficiently unless the archer is strong enough to bring it to full draw. This is necessary to get full action from the limbs. If an archer wants to use a heavy bow he must become strong enough to draw it all the way.

In other words, I find that a bow of, say, thirty-five-pounds pull, if drawn to the head of the arrow, will shoot that arrow faster and farther than a seventy-pound bow will cast the same arrow if drawn only so far as to apply thirty-five pounds of force. The seventy-pound bow will shoot faster, harder, and farther only if drawn all the way to take advantage of its extra strength.

An exception to this observation might be the performance of the medieval crossbow, which was actually drawn only a few inches (five or six) from the braced position to the nut. Perhaps the explanation would be that such a crossbow was so strong—some had pulls of as much as 350 to 1000 pounds at this short draw—that there was still enough energy produced for the weapon to perform satisfactorily.

Mountain sheep head. Note the curvature and twisting of the horn which make it difficult to saw out a bow limb.

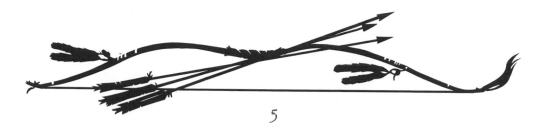

5

# Horn Bows

Of all the bows in America the most fascinating and in some ways the most beautiful were those of horn. They were found on the northern Plains and on the Plateau. They have reportedly been made of elk antler, mountain-sheep horn, and buffalo horn. Some bows of the same class have even been reported to have been made of buffalo ribs. How the Indians came to develop such bows is hard to imagine, but it shows, if nothing else, that archery played a very important role in their lives.

One writer declared that it was because there was a dearth of bow wood in the areas where the horn bow was found. This certainly cannot be the full answer, because the same writer says that of all the "compound bows" those of the Sioux were the most beautiful in shape.[1] The Sioux had a number of good woods available for making bows. Even in the farthest reaches of their territory they still could find ash, chokecherry, serviceberry, wild plum, and crab apple in the wooded areas along the streams in the Dakotas, Wyoming, and Montana which they did use for their wooden bows.

The same thing might be said for the Crows and their relatives the Hidatsas (Gros Ventres or Minitaris), the Arikaras, and for the Nez Perces, who had several other varieties of both hard and soft wood available on the Plateau. One of their favorites was seringa, or mock orange.

Even the Paiutes and Shoshonis had wood for bows, as we have seen, as did the Utes too. They had mountain mahogany, juniper, and perhaps other woods available.

There seems to be no doubt that the horn bow came into prominence after the coming of the horse, when it became necessary to develop short powerful bows to be used when riding. And the Indians must have been somewhat desperate to turn to the materials already named because they were anything but ideal. We have no animal like the water buffalo of Asia for making horn bows; so the Indian bowyers had to do the best they could, using a great deal of imagination, ingenuity, skill, and patience.

With the exception of the Paiutes the Indians who used horn bows were horsemen. Shoshonis were among the first to acquire horses, which they did from their relatives the Comanches farther to the south. And since the Paiutes are also their relatives, living near the southern bands of Shoshonis, they probably borrowed the horn bow from them. Perhaps the biggest reason for owning a horn bow anyway, for horsemen or for anyone, was again prestige, or for the "medicine," as in the owning of a gun. Although there must have been many horn bows at one time, if we are to believe early writers who saw them in operation, they were never as numerous, naturally, as wooden bows. They were comparatively scarce and involved the use of rare materials because just procuring the horns was a feat for only the most experienced hunter, especially when armed with only bow and arrows. Therefore, these little horn bows were valuable and would bring as much as two horses in trade, which also meant that it required prestige to own one; owning one added more prestige.

How the Indians ever came to the conclusion that some kinds of horn could be used for making bows is difficult to tell. Apparently they already had the sinew-backed bow; so it was largely a matter of substituting something for the wood and then building up more sinew than had previously been used. Experiments have shown that horn will stand a great deal of compression but almost no tension, whereas the sinew is excellent under tension. The Oriental bows of horn and sinew have a wooden core with horn glued to the belly and sinew to the back, with the sinew somewhat thicker than the horn.

Having discovered that there was an advantage in using horn, what kind of horn could Indians use? Buffalo, of course, would be the easiest to get, and some reports state that it was used. I cannot believe them. The largest buffalo-bull horns I have ever seen would not be long enough when joined in the center to make even a thirty-inch bow, which is the smallest size of horn bow in existence. The only way it could have been done would have been by splicing the horn in each limb, a delicate and precarious operation, although if well done, the strength of the added sinew and glue might prevent breakage.

Some beautiful horn bows in the National Museum collected in the late 1800s have been pronounced "cow horn," and it would have been possible for Plains and Plateau Indians to get horns from Texas longhorns after the cattle drives to the north. A pair of Texas longhorns would theoretically make a

*Hidatsa Dog Dancer,* by Bodmer, from Prince Maximilian's *Travels.* One of the best illustrations of a horn bow. Courtesy of the Smithsonian Institution, Bureau of American Ethnology.

beautiful bow; some are long enough to make a bow of one horn without a center splice. But experiments by American bowyers using cattle horns have not been satisfactory. The Turks claimed that only the carabao, or water-buffalo, horn, the horn from one type of goat, and that of a type of longhorned cattle south of Constantinople were suitable for bow making.[2]

As far as sinew-backed bows are concerned I feel that the use of sinew for this purpose was discovered in Asia and worked around the world in both directions. It could have come to America in one of the later migrations. We have already pointed out that the bow is fairly recent in this hemisphere and the sinew-backed bow is still more recent. Knowledge of a horn bow could possibly have come from Asia too. Although sinew was not used in the East and Southeast, I do not believe that has anything to do with ignorance of its existence, or with the weather, as has sometimes been implied. It has been said that the climate there is too damp for good use of the sinewed bow. I have used my sinew-backed bows in all these areas, in all kinds of weather, and find almost no "let-down," even in wet weather. The bear or deer fats and oils the Indians used for protecting their equipment from dampness would probably be just as serviceable as the varnish or linseed oil I used on mine. I have soaked a bow for a week in water in order to remove the sinew. Even several hours of soaking barely softened it up. So, to my mind, even a severe wetting would do no great harm. It would, however, quickly affect sinew bowstrings and sinew-wrapped heads and feathers on arrows, which these tribes, as well as most tribes over the country, used.

Therefore, I think that sinew was not used on bows in the East and Southeast only because they did not need it. They were completely satisfied with their longer self bows. They did not even need a bow of the superior cast that the sinew would induce because there was no opportunity to make long shots. Certainly, the climate in these regions is no wetter than it is in some of the coastal regions of California, Oregon, Washington, and British Columbia, where the sinew-backed bow held sway more than in any other locality. Making a sinew-backed bow is a lot of work, and few people, of any race, do any more work than they have to do.

Yet the sinew-backed bow was used to some extent by tribes as far east as the Menomini near the Great Lakes. As mentioned before, they were probably influenced by Plains tribes only a little farther to the west. Although not horse Indians, they recognized a good thing when they saw it. They also used snake skin on the backs of some of their bows, which served as a protection from weather.

I once thought no wood could be used for a short bow of thirty to forty inches length, even with sinew backing, that would be as efficient as horn, unless possibly it were Osage orange, but now I am not so sure. I have seen one horn bow about forty-eight inches long and have heard of another, but by far most of them are under forty inches and many are only about thirty inches long. An average would seem to be about thirty-four inches. I finally was able to make a bow from mountain-sheep horn. It is rather difficult, to put it mildly, to get a pair of trophy horns such as are necessary, but I was lucky enough to have a pair given to me. The period of greatest production and use of horn bows seems to have been the first half of the nineteenth century, and I doubt that any Indian has made a horn bow in the last hundred years or more.

Before I made my horn bow I tried to duplicate one with wood. I used Osage orange because I was convinced it would be best for the purpose. Tests have shown that Osage orange has about the same compressive strength as water-buffalo horn, the favorite of the Turks. So my trial was an Osage bow of 48 inches length, considerably longer than most horn bows but greatly reflexed at the center and with ends turned back on a long curve of about six inches. I trimmed the stave its entire length to a thickness of 7/8 of an inch and 1 3/8 inches wide, smeared the center liberally with bear grease, heated it as hot as I dared over an electric burner, actually until the grease began to smoke, and bent it over a 5-inch log by standing on both ends until cool. I happened to have bear grease on hand, and since it is what the Indians used, I gave it a try. Lard probably would work just as well but would not have as much "medicine."

The coals of an outdoor fire would also do just as well as an electric burner. I know because I have done the same sort of thing out of doors. After roughing out the bow and trimming it to shape, I recurved the ears in much the same way except that I bound them to wooden blocks carved with the desired curve. This kind of ear actually makes a working recurve. I scrubbed and scoured the back of the bow with naphtha soap, then gave it a final scrubbing with a lye solution (Indians used wood ashes) to remove all grease and the natural oil of the Osage orange. After applying a heavy coat of sinew I let the bow hang for a couple of weeks. The result was a bow that shoots as nicely as any I have ever tried. It shoots fast and sweet with no kick or jar. This bow has a total reflex of eight inches when relaxed. Sinew, of course, continues to cure for as much as two years after it is applied and cannot be relied upon for final set until at least six months, although it is safe to shoot the bow in about two weeks (in fact, it may be better to start using it then).

Now I was ready to try my mountain-sheep horn. The two strips cut for the bow were long enough to make a forty-five inch bow and were approximately a quarter of an inch thick all the way. (For cutting the strips, see page 84.) But I had much difficulty in trying to straighten the curled horn strips. Mountain-sheep horns, as you know, are a great open spiral. First I soaked the strips in water for a week; then they softened readily enough in boiling water, even at this altitude of 6,500 feet where water boils at 197 degrees instead of 212. In less than two hours' boiling the strips became almost as soft and flexible as heavy rubber. Although they stiffen fast on cooling, with Gladys's help it was a simple matter to straighten the strips and clamp them to a form I had cut from a board. After letting them cool and dry several days I removed them from the form, but within a few more days both strips had taken a decided curve to the left or, in other words, to one side, apparently to regain their original curl.

I reheated the strips and placed them on the form several times always with the same results, and so I finally decided to use a wood core. If wooden cores were ever used by Indians for either sheep-horn or elk-antler bows it must have been a rare occurrence. It is impossible to tell on a complete bow of good condition without an X-ray, but the horn bows in existence that have been damaged in such a way that their construction can be studied are all without cores. I made the core of Osage orange, which I doubt any Indian would ever have done, for if he could have procured the Osage he probably would not have bothered with the horn. The core did the trick. The problem then was to get an almost perfect gluing surface on both horn and wood, but I discovered the horn works quite easily with files and scrapers.

Before doing any gluing I gave the Osage orange a lye wash on both sides to take off the natural oil. From then on it had to be handled with great care for even touching it with the hands would likely prevent the glue from adhering properly.

Since the Osage core was of one piece, it solved another problem, that of joining the horn strips. I merely butted them together at the center and glued them to the belly side of the core with grade-A hide glue, clamping wood and horn together on the form and letting the bow set for one month. The results seemed to be nearly perfect.

Next I cut the bow to shape. It is 1 3/32 inches wide at the handle, 1 5/32 inches just each side of the handle, and tapered to 9/16 inch at the ends where the nocks are. The wood core is 13/32 inch thick at the handle, which is 4 inches long, tapered to 5/32 inch at midlimb, and to 7/64 at the tips.

I added a heavy coating of moose sinew to the back, going completely over the sides so that only the surface of the horn is exposed. The bow is rectangular in cross section, as most Sioux bows are, even those made of horn. The nocks I built up of sinew, as on most horn bows. When dry the sinew was approximately 5/32 inch thick over the entire bow, but it was at least twice as thick when it was applied moist.

I let the sinew set for two weeks before final tillering and shooting and wrapped the ends and center with buffalo sinew. Just above the center of each limb I added about a three-inch wrapping of deer sinew. So this is a real "medicine" bow—mountain-sheep horn, moose, buffalo and deer sinew, *lila wakan.*

Actually I had very little tillering to do, just scraping the horn belly a little either side of the handle to improve the arc there and that was all.

The results of the shooting were rather disappointing. I have sinew-backed Osage-orange bows of similar size and strength that seem quite a bit snappier. So I cut the horn bow back to a length of forty inches and found great improvement. Therefore, I believe the principal advantage of the horn is in being able to make such a short bow. We all know that the more bend we can give to a short limb, the more efficient is the cast.

The Osage orange alone may be just as good in some respects, but there are other advantages to the horn. First of all, horn was easier to get by most of the Indians who used it than was Osage orange. Another advantage is that no matter how much sinew is built up on a horn foundation the horn will not crack or split, which often happens with any kind of wood when adding sinew enough to develop a deep reflex or to protect such a short bow from breakage through overdraw.

To learn more about this I made a bow of the same size of Osage orange similar to the one already described, but only forty inches long and even more heavily backed with sinew. It turned out to be a beautiful little bow, draws more than seventy pounds at twenty-three inches, and stands this over-draw with no complaints. This is one of my lucky bows and has developed no belly cracks. But I did take the precaution of gluing thin rawhide on the belly before sinewing the back. This rawhide was removed after about six months. It may have prevented cracks; so I think it a good idea and good insurance against cracking. At any rate, the bow is now several years old, as strong and peppy as ever, and still has no cracks. It far outshoots the mountain-sheep bow, although, of course, the mountain-sheep bow is not nearly as strong, and this wooden one was much easier to make. Perhaps it might have been possible to make the sheep-horn bow stronger by cutting the strips wider and thicker, but there are limitations in the structure of the horn that did not make this seem feasible.

Following this experiment I took one of Eagle Hawk's little bows of ash, forty-one inches long, and reshaped it like the Osage orange just mentioned—much reflexed at the center and the ends turned up in a short recurve—then added much sinew to it, again with no belly cracks. It will withstand a twenty-three-inch draw and is a beautifully shaped, snappy little weapon, but not nearly as strong as the one of Osage orange. Its performance compares very well with that of my mountain-sheep bow. All of which brings me further to the conclusion that the horn bows were not made entirely for practical purposes, although they were serviceable. I was really amazed that the little sinew-backed ash bow behaved so well, as I had rather expected it to break under such strain, even with all the sinew backing.

Having gone this far, I decided to try a Turkish bow. Although there is not much resemblance to an Indian bow except in length, my interest in short bows naturally led me to an admiration of these marvelous little examples of the bow maker's art. As already mentioned, Osage orange has been tested as comparable to water-buffalo horn for compression qualities. So I made a Turkish-style bow I now call my "Osage Turk," using a forty-five-inch stave of prime Osage as a starter, with the wood itself to take the place of both wood core and horn belly.

Turkish archery attained its fullest development during a period of a little more than one hundred years between 1450 and 1570, at the very time firearms were being introduced. It continued as a sport until about 1840, and Turkish archers were unrivaled anywhere else in the world. But from about 1800 on few Turkish bowyers remained, and most of the bows still in use were from an earlier period. Today the "newest" Turkish bow still in existence must be close to two hundred years old, and yet some of these have been shot within recent years.

After shaping the bow I turned ears of about 4 1/2 inches; and tillering to a few inches of draw, I then reflexed the entire bow about 8 inches before applying sinew. I also glued a thin strip of rawhide to the belly and let it dry a couple of days before backing the bow heavily with sinew. When dried the sinew was 3/16 inch thick, or about one-third the thickness of the entire bow. Then I let the bow hang by a string across the tips for nearly a year. (Turks spent five to ten years on a bow.) By this time it was reflexed to a depth of 10 7/8 inches and was only 31 3/4 inches across from tip to tip! After removing the rawhide from the belly and doing some minor tillering I braced the bow by bending it across my knees and having Gladys attach the string.

It bent nicely but a little too much toward the ends for a true Turk. So I added more sinew to each end, beginning about twelve inches below the nocks, with a high center ridge from the ears running into the "shoulders." This time I did not put rawhide on the belly, and sure enough, some slight cracks developed beneath the new sinew, which again proved to me that it is a good idea to use the rawhide during the curing process.

Eventually I considered the bow ready for finishing, so I added new rawhide to the belly, not just to hide the cracks, and painted it black to look like carabao horn on a real Turkish bow. I glued a very thin black skive leather on the back, painted a design in gilt on it, then went over the entire bow lightly with cedar oil. (The Turks used sandalwood oil.)

Now I have a bow that looks quite like a Turkish one—not quite as reflexed as some—and so far it is behaving well. I have not tried it for distance, and it may not shoot half a mile like some of the Turkish ones did, but it certainly is fast, and I am learning how to handle it. Maybe the Osage is not as good as the water-buffalo horn, but it seems to be a reasonable substitute. The experiment was satisfying, and in looks the bow is a beauty. Altogether it was a year and a half from start to finish. I checked measurements nearly every day during this period.

In making the "Osage Turk" the wooden bow itself was reflexed to measure 40 3/8 inches across the tips. After the final layer of sinew had cured for nearly a year, the bow had reflexed to 31 inches across the tips. After bracing and shooting for an hour or so, however, the reflex opened to about 34 1/4 inches. Within an hour it had gone back to 31 7/8 inches. Both weather and use affect the reflex, but even in the wettest weather it has never opened up to more than 34 5/8 inches relaxed—37 after use—then takes perhaps 24 hours to come back to 34 or 34 1/4 inches. For a long time the bow did not go back to 31 inches; it apparently had lost a bit of its pent-up power. It occasionally went back to 32 inches, and the average seems to be about 33 1/8. I wondered if it would go back to 31 inches when our cooler weather set in. To my surprise and delight it went back to 30 1/4 inches!

Other sinew-backed bows react to weather and use in similar fashion, but as stated before, they never become flabby, and they respond well in wet weather. Any bow, sinew-backed or not, tends to be stronger and snappier in cold weather and less strong and a trifle slower in hot weather, but with mine, at least, the differences are so slight as to be almost unnoticeable. They are good bows, regardless of weather.

Most sinew-backed bows have been termed "lined" because the sinew is so thin. As previously mentioned, however, even such a thin "lining" practically eliminates breakage, which was doubtless the original reason for using sinew. It also adds considerable strength to the bow. When the sinew is built up to as much as a third of the total thickness of the bow, the resulting reflex and power are tremendous, although the wood on the belly usually develops alarming cracks, which, as I have said, led to my using rawhide on the belly and suggesting that canvas or another non-stretch material might also be used as a preventive. For all their evil appearance, however, I have not yet found that such cracks affect the performance of a bow. Horn may have been used to eliminate them, and this may be one of the reasons the Turks and Orientals came to use horn, because there is no wood in that part of the world that approaches Osage orange for bow wood, and even Osage orange will crack badly at times when heavily backed with sinew. Why it does not always do so must be because of differing qualities of individual staves. Some Indian horn bows had sinew of the same thickness as the horn or even greater. The idea that sinew does nothing but protect the bow from breaking is ridiculous. It definitely adds power and cast, even when used sparingly.

One writer saw a Flathead bow collected about 1868 that was highly reflexed with a snake-skin-covered back and cedar belly and decided it had been made not to shoot but to sell to some gullible white man. He did not think it possible to have so much reflex in anything but an elk-horn bow. This bow doubtless had a sinew back under the snake skin, but he could not have had much experience with sinew because, as I have already said, the sinew alone if thick enough will reflex a bow. If the stave is reflexed first before the sinew is applied, it will not only hold that reflex but will draw it even deeper. The above-mentioned writer had the idea that if the sinew was too thick in relation to the wood the wood cells would collapse and the bow limbs would follow the string.

In actuality, almost the exact opposite takes place. The wooden belly may crack lengthwise and sometimes even chrysal under the tension of the sinew, but the reflex will not only be maintained but may become deeper with time. The idea that any Indian would go to all the work necessary to make such a fine-looking bow, even though a wooden one, just to palm off on some unsuspecting white man, perhaps in place of a horn bow for which he was looking, is hard to accept. To fake a bow just by gluing a snake skin over a reflexed wooden back, which of course would be impractical for shooting, is just too much to believe.

The few Indian bows of mountain-sheep horn I have been privileged to examine definitely had the outside of the horn as the face, or outside surface of the belly. The heavy ridges in the native horn had been carefully cut, scraped, and sanded away to a nice smooth surface, but it was still evident that it was the outside of the horn. The lateral, or thickness, taper of the horn limbs is so slight as to be almost negligible, but what tapering and trimming had been done was certainly done on the inner side before sinewing, and the sinew had been applied to this same surface. All the Indian horn bows I have seen, or seen in pictures, were at least slightly reflexed and some quite highly so, but never to the extent found in the Oriental bows.

The tillering otherwise was done through the tapering of the limbs as observed from the back or the belly, and it runs from widths near the grip of 1 and 1 1/2 inches to 1/4 and 1/2 inch at the tips. Some tillering could also be accomplished by laying the sinew on a little thinner toward the tips, but in checking one of these little bows with calipers the taper on the sides was only 1/16 inch from grip to center limb and remained constant from there to the tips.

This little mountain-sheep bow is from the Vernon collection in the Colter Bay Museum in Grand Teton National Park. We were able to have it X-rayed to learn more about its construction. The bow is slightly oval in cross section and is only 30 7/8 inches long, 1 1/8 inches wide at the grip, 9/16 inch thick at the grip, and 1/2 inch at the nocks, which are slightly built up of sinew with a nice little recurve of about an inch at the tips. They are ornamental only. The bow is 15/32 inch wide at the nocks, measured over a thin wrapping of sinew at the ends. The horn is 3/8 inch thick at the center, 5/16 inch at midlimb, and continues the same thickness to the nocks. The sinew is 3/16 inch thick, apparently all the way from nock to nock. The tips of the horn are only about 1/4 inch thick but, as mentioned above, nicely bent for the foundation of the tiny recurve. The sinew from the back completely surrounds these tips, then the ends are wrapped with flat sinew for about 3 inches.

The bow was once reflexed about 3 inches, but one limb now "follows the string" quite badly. The good limb has a suggestion of a slight recurve toward the end. The X-ray showed the reason for the string follow. It had been broken and patched. The break was on a slight angle and had been repaired by drilling two holes, about an inch apart, through which hand-forged nails had been run and crimped over on the belly side. To make such a repair the sinew had to be soaked off first, then glued back in place. The final repair was to wrap the limb over the break with a thin band of sinew for about three inches.

Such was the esteem in which these little bows were held that someone went to all this trouble to make this repair, even though it could not possibly perform as well afterward as it had before the break.

This bow is listed as coming from the Crows but is the same in appearance as some Nez Perce sheep-horn bows. Crows and Nez Perces have exchanged ideas for many years. One Nez Perce bow I have seen is thirty-six inches long, with the lower limb a little shorter than the upper. It has a piece of buckskin sewed on the handle decorated at each end with bands of seed beads.

Our first interest in X-raying the bow was to learn how it was joined at the center, for as it hung in the glass display case this could not be observed. As soon as the bow was removed from the case it was evident that the horn was one single piece. The record for such a one-piece horn bow, as far as I know, is thirty-eight inches. Wouldn't that be a trophy head!

To get back to cow-horn bows: I think the so-called cow-horn bows may also be of mountain-sheep horn, but worked down completely through the outer layer, so that all evidences of the heavy ridges natural to the horn are erased. In making my sheep-horn bow I said I tillered it by lightly scraping the limbs, just as I would in making a wooden bow. After a final polishing most people who see it think it is cattle horn.

Although mountain-sheep horn would seem to be anything but an ideal material for a bow, it softens readily in boiling water, as has already been pointed out. But buffalo horn will not soften enough to shape even at 212 degrees. To soften buffalo horn I have had to use a solution of half water and half glycerin in order to bend it readily, and I am convinced it will not make a bow because it is too short and too brittle.

The preliminary work of cutting the strips from a mountain-sheep horn is the biggest problem. Three band-saw blades were broken in sawing out the horns I used. Without modern tools it must have been an enormous job and with only stone and bone tools, a seemingly impossible one. As far as I know, no remains of horn bows have ever been found in prehistoric sites, although other objects of bone, horn, and even wood have sometimes been recovered. Before they had ever seen a white man, western Indians had obtained a few metal tools, through barter or conquest, from other tribes who had had first-hand contact with Whites. Very early they acquired such things as hatchets, knives, saws, and files. Without such tools the making of horn bows must have been rare or nonexistent. Since we think the horn bow developed after the coming of the horse, the tools to make them likewise would be forthcoming from the same source.

The strips for the bow must come from the very center, or flat outer surface, of the curled horn. This makes sawing or any other kind of cutting difficult, but with time and care it can be accomplished. The strips I used were 1 3/32 inches wide at their widest, and, as already mentioned, about 1/4 inch thick. I smoothed off the heavy cross ridges before boiling the strips, but it might have been just as well to have removed them after they were boiled and straightened.

The horn-bow country is also generally the country of natural hot springs. I think that soaking the entire horn in one of these hot springs would soften it enough that it might even be worked with stone tools. The horn can be cut with any degree of ease only while it is hot; so the soaking would have to be renewed every few minutes, and depending upon the degree of heat in the pool, the horn would have to be left in for a shorter or longer period each time it was worked.

Indians often softened wood by burying it in a trench, pouring boiling water over it, then building a fire on top of the filled-in trench for as long as twenty-four hours. The same process might have been used for horn, but the hot spring would be better. Indians often traveled many miles to receive the therapeutic benefits of natural hot springs; so there is no reason why they would not do likewise for more tangible results, such as making a horn bow.

After boiling, the horn had to be set on some kind of form to straighten and shape it. This could be done by carving a form of wood and binding the horn to it, or by staking it to the ground.

The horn bows I have seen have been reflexed either by bending a single piece at the center or by setting back the joint at the handle, or grip. Even a wooden stave treated in this fashion is almost bound to make a double-curved bow. The only exception would be to keep the handle straight and reflex each limb in a long, graceful curve beyond it. It has been stated by some writers that a double-curved bow is not as efficient as a single-curved bow, sometimes called a "D" bow, and that the Indians "deformed" the bow for some unknown, impractical reason, but my own experience over many years of experimenting convinces me that there is much advantage in a double-curved bow, even when the limbs themselves may follow the string. Such a bow still has the advantage of a reflexed center, and of course, that advantage is the extra energy stored in the limbs which increases the tension on the bow string and is released when the string is released. Given two bows of the same wood, same size, and same quality of workmanship, one double-curved, the other single-curved, the double-curved bow will shoot harder and faster.

Some double-curved bows spring in the handle because it is not built rigid enough. Such bows may have good cast because of the extra action in the handle section, but are usually mean to shoot because they kick. I have never known a double-curved bow with a stiff handle to kick. Of course kick, or jar, can come from poor tillering, or from having the tips too heavy, but in the case of bows of Indian design the worst kickers were those with flexible handles. However, Indians were not interested in target shooting, but in getting meat or in defending themselves against enemies.

Indians, at least in some areas, certainly had discovered the principle of the reflexed bow of storing more energy in the relaxed bow, so that when braced it had extra cast and power. The belief held by some people that a single end-to-end curve is more efficient does not make sense. Even the makers of English-style longbows learned long ago that a bow could be improved by using a spliced stave made of two joined billets and setting the handle back somewhat. They apparently stumbled upon this by accident because of the difficulty of obtaining the best bow woods—yew and Osage orange—in long enough pieces for a self bow. Once they began splicing two billets together, it became obvious that by setting back the handle a certain amount of string follow would be eliminated. The resulting bow was bound to be one with a slightly reflexed center and double-curved limbs. At the same time it was a better bow because with less string follow there was more stored energy, as in other reflexed or recurved bows.

As mentioned before, among the Indian bows and Indian-style bows I have handled, the worst offenders for kicking were those with flexible handles. Others of these double-curved bows have had a slight, but not really objectionable, jar, which actually was not nearly as severe as that of any short single-curved bow. As anyone knows, a short plain or single-curved bow stacks tremendously. That is, it takes much more effort to pull the bow towards the end of the draw than it did at the beginning. Much of this stack is eliminated in the double-curved bow. It can be completely eliminated if the ends are adequately recurved.

Most horn bows have a slight recurve at the ends, which must have increased their shooting qualities to some extent. In my early experiments with sinew I discovered that, if a bow is well tillered before applying the sinew and then has enough sinew added, the tension of the sinew as it dries not only will add considerable reflex to a perfectly straight bow but will add slight recurves to the ends, which thus serve as the working recurves we often hear about.

Maximilian, as well as Catlin, reported horn bows among the Blackfeet. Ralph Hubbard, well-known authority on Indian lore and crafts, wrote to me that he had once examined a Blackfoot bow of mountain-sheep horn many years ago. He remembered it as being at least four feet long, exceptional for a horn bow, with the usual reflexed center and double curves. He was told that the Blackfeet sometimes used a core of ash. A wooden core of almost any kind would facilitate the manufacture of a horn bow, as I found out, not only helping to keep the bow in line but also making it easier to join the horn strips at the handle.

Hubbard's Blackfoot friend told him that the horn was boiled for hours and hours, then pounded with a stone maul until strips of horn could be pulled off six to eight inches long. These were later glued to the core, on the belly side, overlapping the ends much as the sinew itself is overlapped on the back. The glue was made by boiling hoofs of deer, antelope, or elk. Altogether, he described it as quite a messy, fussy operation and thought that making one such bow in a lifetime would be sufficient. It seems to me that if bows were ever made this way a great deal of unnecessary work was involved. Just cutting full-length strips from the horn would be enough of a task but easier than all this. The final polishing was done with pumice stone, obtained from the Yellowstone Park region, and sandstone.

Hubbard was also told that the Kutenais made horn bows. We know, of course, that most horn bows still in existence were apparently made of horn and sinew with no wooden core.

A pretty little bow in the Jefferson Memorial Museum in Saint Louis, made of mountain-sheep horn, is about thirty-five inches long with a nice center reflex and a suggestion of a recurve at the tips. The nocks are built up of sinew; the handle and a section of each limb are decorated with red flannel wrapped with thongs decorated with porcupine quills. Most horn bows are decorated in some such fashion.

Recently I made another big horn bow. This time I sawed the strips from the horns by hand using a coping saw. It took longer but it was easier to gauge results. The finished bow is 38 1/2 inches long from tip to tip, measured along the belly. This time it is a true Indian-type with no wood core. The horn strips are 1 3/8 inches wide at the center and 1/2 inch wide at the tips. They are 12/32 inch thick near the grip, 11/32 inch at midlimb, 21/64 inch near the tips. The sinew on the finished bow is approximately 9/32 inch thick. So far the bow is keeping in line and looks beautiful. It is much stronger than the first one. In fact, it was an awful job to string it and it must pull at least eighty pounds. Yet the proportions I used are in keeping with other horn bows. It would be interesting if one such bow could still be strung and tested for comparison.

Lewis and Clark reported bows of elk horn among the tribes they visited, but said those of "the bighorn are still more prized, and are formed by cementing with glue flat pieces of the horn together, covering the back with sinews and glue, and loading the whole with an unusual quantity of ornaments.[3] By "flat pieces" I think the reference is to two pieces, or strips, joined together at the handle rather than to any splicing to build up the limbs as in the Blackfoot bow mentioned above or the buffalo horn bow mentioned earlier.

Many writers since Lewis and Clark have reported bows of elk horn, although none ever gave complete details of how they were made. I had always doubted that elk antler was actually used for bows. Although tests have shown that it has great strength under compression, it just seemed too hard and brittle. And tests I have made proved to me that neither mountain-sheep horn nor antler can be used alone. They must be backed with sinew to endow them with the necessary tensile strength to withstand the extreme bending. It is not too difficult to cut the antler with a hacksaw—and plenty of patience and time. The antler was supposed to have been softened and straightened with heat in using a trench with water and a fire on top, as has already been described. But in the tests I have made with boiling elk antler it does not soften nearly as readily as mountain-sheep horn. Also, the few bows I have been able to examine closely looked more like bone than antler, although elk antler will take a nice polish and small pieces when polished look like bone.

A Hidatsa bow I have seen supposedly made of elk horn is four feet long, and the upper end, which in this case is the tied end, is nearly six inches longer than the lower end. It has a sinewed back covered with snake skin. The extra length of the upper limb may be due to wrapping a handle about six inches below center, beginning at the center, as the central portion of the bow has no taper.

I wondered for a long time if such bows were not really made of baleen, or whale bone, because long ago I read that medieval crossbows, before steel ones were developed, were made of whale bone and sinew. Although I have seen no reference to the West Coast Indians using baleen for bows, they were great whalers, and they procured whale bone for other purposes. Mention has been made of trade routes up and down and all across the country. West Coast dentalium shells and abalone shells reached tribes far inland, and there is no reason to think that baleen could not have been a trade item also.

In rereading the Catlin books I rediscovered his surmises on this same subject. Writing of Indian bows, he stated:

There are very many also (among the Blackfeet and the Crows) which are made of bone, and others of the horn of the mountain sheep. Those made of bone are decidedly the most valuable, and cannot in this country, be procured of a good quality short of the price of one or two horses. About them there is a mystery yet to be solved, and I advance my opinion against all theories that I have heard in the country where they are used and made. I have procured several very fine specimens, and when purchasing them have inquired of the Indians, what bone they were made of? and in every instance, the answer was, "That's medicine," meaning that it was a mystery to them, or that they did not wish to be questioned about them. The bone of which they are made is certainly not the bone of any animal now grazing on the prairies or in the mountains between this place and the Pacific Ocean; for some of these bows are three feet in length, of a solid piece of bone, and that as close-grained—as hard—as white, and as highly polished as any ivory; it cannot, therefore, be made from the elk's horn (as some have supposed), which is of a dark colour and porous; nor can it come from the buffalo. It is my opinion, therefore, that the Indians on the Pacific coast procure the bone from the jaw of the sperm whale which is often stranded on that coast, and bring the bone into the mountains, trade it to the Blackfeet and Crows, who manufacture it into these bows without knowing any more than we do, from what source it has been procured.[4]

It is interesting that Catlin said these bone bows were worth more than those of mountain-sheep horn, whereas Lewis and Clark stated just the opposite. Previously Catlin had said that the Indian bows were short (he was then at the mouth of the Yellowstone River), from 2 1/2 to 3 feet long, which was a "size more easily and handily used on horseback than one of greater length." He said they were usually made of ash or of *bois d'arc* (Osage orange) "and lined on the back with layers of buffalo or deer's sinews, which are inseparably attached to them, and give them great elasticity." Then he told of the "bone" bows, which implies to me that they were also "lined" with sinew. Some one has said that Catlin was gullible, but his story makes more sense to me than some of the others that tell of the elk horn bows.

George Belden wrote that the Crows made bows of elk horn, saying:

They take a large horn or prong and saw a slice off each side of it; these slices are then filed or rubbed down until the flat sides fit nicely together, when they are glued and wrapped at the ends. Four slices made a bow, it being jointed. Another piece of horn is laid on the center of the bow at the grasp, where it is glued fast. The whole is then filed down until it is perfectly proportioned, when the white bone is ornamented, carved and painted. Nothing can exceed the beauty of these bows, and it takes an Indian about three months to make one. They are very expensive, and the Indians do not sell them; but I managed to get one from a friend for thirty-two dollars in gold.[5]

He says nothing about sinew, although he gives a partial description of the sinew-backed wooden bow, and he says nothing as to how the antler was straightened and shaped. Furthermore, he said, "They . . . saw a slice off each side of it," which is an impossibility on any antler I have ever seen because one would always have the prongs, or tines, to contend with on the opposite side of the slice.

He did not say why they needed four pieces of horn and did not say much about how they were put together. He may never have seen one made but merely tried to relate how it was explained to him. He may have thought the sinew back was an extra slice of horn. Getting one slice of antler with modern equipment is task enough. I doubt very much they could or would obtain two strips for each limb. Two strips glued together as Belden stated would give adequate thickness to the bow limbs, but the bow would still have to be heavily backed with sinew, and as far as I have been able to learn, the existing bows seem to be made of solid pieces of "bone." The limbs are not laminated, but they are all sinew-backed. Tests I made proved to me that neither mountain-sheep horn nor antler can be used alone. They must be backed with sinew to endow them with the necessary tensile strength to withstand the extreme bending.

There may have been several methods of making horn bows, and at this late date it is almost impossible to find out more about them.

Belden also said he had "seen a bow throw an arrow five hundred yards," which is a sizeable distance. He could hardly have meant five hundred feet, for there would be nothing exceptional in that.

One writer stated that the tines of the antlers were chopped off with a butcher knife. I would like to see anyone chop them off with a butcher knife, or even with an ax! Indians have been known to make a saw from an old butcher knife, or even from a table knife, and they possibly could have sawed the tines off with such a tool. But why go to all the trouble of removing the tines? They would not be in the way because only the smooth side of the antler, with no tines, could possibly be used for bow material. I think that even the meager reports available on making elk horn bows were written by men who never actually saw it done, and who did not even know enough about bow building to set down correctly what little information they did gather about their construction.

I picked up two freshly dropped antlers and decided to saw out strips for a bow, even if it took me a year, and find out just what kind of a bow they would make. The two freshly dropped antlers were of comparable size but it is next to impossible to find a pair from the same animal. He may shed one antler in one place and the other hours, sometimes days, later and probably miles away. Although this "pair" I picked up were closely alike in length and shape I was sure one was from a younger animal than the other. The one I considered older was slightly heavier and rougher.

I know of no way to make an elk horn bow except to shape the horn somehow in order to make it usable. Meager reports, written in the days when Indians were still making horn bows, state that the necessary strips of horn were sawed off, then boiled until soft in order to shape them. The horn as provided by the elk even on its straightest side is certainly much too crooked for the limb of a bow.

With as coarse-bladed a hack saw as I could get I sawed off a strip from each antler about half an inch thick and twenty-three inches long (it took about fifteen minutes to saw one inch). I intended to lap the strips at the handle and make a bow forty inches long because I thought that length would be about average. It is the length of my mountain-sheep horn bow.

I boiled the strips for an hour (I used a fifty-fifty solution of Prestone and water to try to raise the boiling point at this high altitude). Still as stiff as when first sawed off. I boiled them three more hours. Still stiff as ever. I boiled them twelve hours. Then I got results. The pithy center had softened to a kind of mush, and the first strip I took out of the boiling water shaped quite easily and very well to the wooden form (the same form used for the mountain-sheep horn). I was elated, but when I tried the same procedure with the other strip it broke in half a dozen pieces!

The strip that came out well was from the antler of the older animal and about which I had been quite doubtful. My conclusion is that if Indians made antler bows it must have taken considerable experience to choose which antlers to use or not to use. Apparently the antlers from the older animals would be the ones to choose, but not too old, as I imagine the antlers from an extremely old bull would not do either. The best way to make a choice would be to select the animal on the hoof rather than take a chance on finding a matched pair of freshly dropped horns.

Working with the kind of antlers I had it would be necessary to use very thin strips. Measurements that have been reported of the antler section of a bow being 3/8 to 1/2 an inch in thickness near the grip cannot possibly be from such an antler, or at least not from one layer. As already stated, the bows that can still be examined all seem to be one layer of horn. No elk antler that I have ever examined has had a hard outer part more than 1/4 inch thick and that only near the base. About 3/16 is average for the remaining length. The sketches I made to illustrate cross sections of horn bows were drawn according to dimensions given, but I still think it impossible to find elk horn as thick as some of the drawings show. If the dimensions given were correct, the bows must have been of some other material, or were from much larger antlers than I have been able to procure. I do not believe that even two layers such as Belden reported could be cut so as to give dimensions as large as some of those shown in the drawings. One would be lucky to produce a bow of as much as 1 1/4 inches by 1/2 inch at the handle, even by laminating two strips of antler.

According to my own experiments and experience with elk horn only a very small bow could be produced, not over 1 1/8 by 15/16 inches at the handle and 15/16 by 1/2 inch at midlimb—total measurements, including sinew.

Of the sketches I made, in my opinion the Hidatsa bow could not possibly be elk antler, and even the Arikara, Crow, and Paiute bows would require antlers heavier than any I have worked with. The antlers I used were from 41 to 49 inches long and about 6 inches in circumference at the base, average size for fully matured animals. The largest elk antlers ever recorded are a little over 64 inches and 9 3/4 inches in circumference. An Indian hunter looking for bow material would usually have to be content with something much smaller, similar to what I used.

Another thing, some "elk horn" bows are reportedly made of a single piece with no splice at the handle. However, although almost any elk antler would be long enough for a bow, it has so many angles and curves that I doubt even heat and boiling would ever enable one to make a bow of a single piece. At least I have never been able to do it. Baleen, on the other hand, would be long enough and straight enough for any of the bows to be seen in museums today and, backed with sinew, should be serviceable. (Baleen appears to be black, but is white after the thin outer covering is removed.)

The inner, pithy part of the antler is worthless for any kind of a bow if it has to be boiled, for as I have stated, it becomes mushy with enough boiling to soften the antler sufficiently for shaping. When this "mush" is scraped away, a rounded shell of not over one-fourth inch of hard material is left. With softening and pressing this might be nearly flattened, but I have not been able to flatten it to any extent, and I have more sophisticated equipment than Indians had. On drying, after the rough outer surface has been ground and polished, it looks much like bone.

It is possible to fill the concave center of the limb with sinew, then build up more sinew over this all the way to the sides of the bow, lapping even slightly onto the belly. The outer side of the horn is definitely used for the belly of the bow.

There is no doubt that elk antler will stand a great deal of compression, and we know that sinew will stand much tension. If these materials are used together, the outside of the horn must be the belly, and the inner side, with pith removed, must take the sinew.

A possible exception to the above statements about the pithy center of the horn may be the Eskimo bows. I have had no opportunity to examine carefully an Eskimo horn bow, but from illustrations in Mason's report, first published in 1893, it looks as if reindeer antler was used "as is," with the porous center as the back of the bow, reinforced with sinew cord. Apparently the antler was not boiled to straighten it out; otherwise the porous part would have disintegrated. (In earlier times, the Eskimo had no way of boiling anything as large as a reindeer horn and in most parts of their country could not even have used a trench, as the Indians did.) Consequently, the limbs are quite crooked, having been selected from the straightest possible antlers and left at that. Compared to some of the beautiful horn or antler bows of the Indians, the Eskimo antler bow was a crude contrivance, although the result of much time, patience, and ingenuity.

I found another pair of elk antlers and tried again. This time I produced a real elk horn bow. I wondered if, after all the work, the horn would have sufficient elasticity to be a good bow, although it did have quite a bit of spring. I did not try to bend it to any extent, however, for even though I knew it would stand considerable compression, I had no doubt it would break without the sinew that was to be applied to it, and this would not be a fair test.

Both strips withstood the boiling and clamping to the form, and on being released several days later, showed no sign of warping or returning to their original shape. I made a slight lap at the handle, then glued another piece of antler cut to fit, about four inches long, above the splice on the back side. When the glue had dried, I wrapped the entire handle section heavily with sinew strips, also set in glue, then reclamped the whole thing back on the form and let it set for about a week.

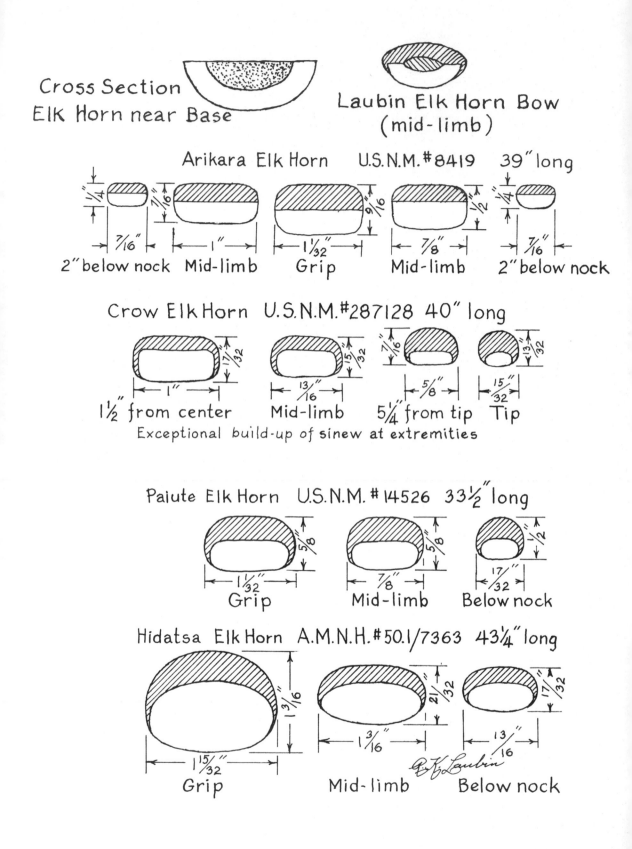

Cross Section
Elk Horn near Base

Laubin Elk Horn Bow
(mid-limb)

Arikara Elk Horn    U.S.N.M. #8419    39" long

2" below nock    Mid-limb    Grip    Mid-limb    2" below nock

Crow Elk Horn    U.S.N.M. #287128    40" long

1½" from center    Mid-limb    5¼" from tip    Tip

Exceptional build-up of sinew at extremities

Paiute Elk Horn    U.S.N.M. #14526    33½" long

Grip    Mid-limb    Below nock

Hidatsa Elk Horn    A.M.N.H. #50.1/7363    43¼" long

Grip    Mid-limb    Below nock

## Ute Mountain Sheep Horn  U.S.N.M. #203812  38" long

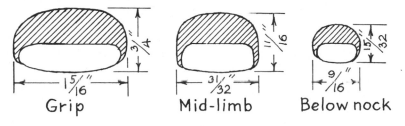

Grip $1\frac{5}{16}''$ — $\frac{3}{4}''$

Mid-limb $\frac{31}{32}''$ — $\frac{11}{16}''$

Below nock $\frac{9}{16}''$ — $\frac{15}{32}''$

## Crow-Vernon Coll. Mountain Sheep Horn  $30\frac{7}{8}''$ long

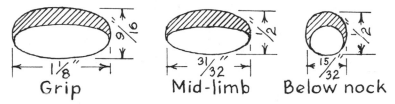

Grip $1\frac{1}{8}''$ — $\frac{9}{16}''$

Mid-limb $\frac{31}{32}''$ — $\frac{1}{2}''$

Below nock $\frac{15}{32}''$ — $\frac{1}{2}''$

## Laubin Mountain Sheep Horn, wood core  40" long

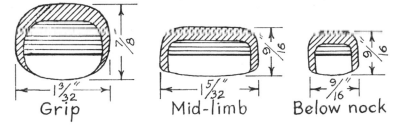

Grip $1\frac{3}{32}''$ — $\frac{7}{8}''$

Mid-limb $1\frac{5}{32}''$ — $\frac{9}{16}''$

Below nock $\frac{9}{16}''$ — $\frac{9}{16}''$

## Nez Perce Mountain Sheep Horn  A.M.N.H. #1/2707  $37\frac{3}{4}''$ long

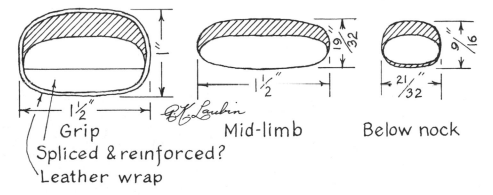

Grip $1\frac{1}{2}''$  
Spliced & reinforced?  
Leather wrap

Mid-limb $1\frac{1}{2}''$ — $\frac{19}{32}''$

Below nock $\frac{21}{32}''$ — $\frac{9}{16}''$

Cross sections of horn bows in the American Museum of Natural History and the United States National Museum. The sinew is indicated by crosshatching. Dimensions from T. M. Hamilton, *Native American Bows.*

For sinew I used caribou given to me by a friend from Alaska. First I filled the concave center with sinew; then I laid a very heavy layer over this all the way to the edge and a bit over the sides, as mentioned above, and also brought it up over the tips and onto the belly side as in most Indian bows; and I built up sinew nocks.

On the form the limbs were reflexed to a distance across the tips of 36 3/4 inches, a pretty good reflex on a 40-inch bow. After a few days of curing, upon taking the bow off the form it immediately further reflexed to 32 inches! At the end of two weeks I decided to string the bow. It was an exciting time! Now I would find out whether one could really make a bow of elk antler, or whether all my time, interest, and effort had been wasted.

The little bow at first seemed much stronger than I had anticipated. It took all my strength to bring the limbs back to bracing position but it behaved beautifully. Carefully I brought the limbs around, and Gladys placed the string over the sinew nocks. The shape was a beautiful double curve, almost perfect. Since I had made a special effort to put equal amounts of sinew on each limb but had no way of tillering the limbs beforehand, I filed a couple of places on the horn belly of one limb that were not quite true, and then the bow was ready.

But now that it was strung it did not seem strong at all. It seems most of the strength was in the reflex. It had good spring but was much too light to suit me. I shot a few arrows with it and was disappointed with their speed. It was hardly more than a child's bow.

My next move was to add another heavy layer of sinew on the bow in an effort to strengthen it. About two months later the reflex had deepened so much that the bow was now twenty-nine inches across the tips, and so strong now that I could not bend it enough to get a string on it. I kept working it a little each day, bending it across my knees in an effort to limber it up. Eventually I did get it bent enough to put a string on it, but while I was straining to hold it in position and Gladys was trying to put the string in place, all of a sudden there was a loud CRACK! and the bow broke just above the handle, splintering badly for about three inches. That temporarily ended my experiment.

I do not quite understand why one limb broke, after having strung and shot the bow before adding the new sinew. It would seem that the extra sinew would be extra protection against breakage, but such was not the case. Another thought comes to mind. I now think that the reflex may have been so great that the antler was already bent to its limit while trying to string the bow. But why did one limb break and not the other one? In fact, the good limb will still stand

Flying Cloud, or Mahpiya Kinyeyapi (Judge Frank Zahn), the authors' interpreter, at Fort Yates, North Dakota.

a lot more bending with no complaint. Part of the trouble must be in the quality of the antlers themselves. The one that broke might have been damaged in such a way that microscopic cracks caused the breakage under the greater tension of extra sinew and extra reflex.

Not even two pieces of wood are ever alike. Two beautiful staves may look identical, but one may make a good bow and the other may not. For instance, a little tree growing in what seemed like an ideal spot, with plenty of moisture and well protected, turned out a stave of poor quality, while one growing up a little draw in a dry and hostile environment produced a good one. Its very struggle for existence may have contributed to its toughness and flexibility.

I still hardly know what to say about elk horn bows. I am now convinced that there could be and was such a thing, but I lean toward Catlin's theory. From all my efforts I have come to the following conclusions: I feel certain now that Indians seldom, if ever, used dropped antlers unless lucky enough to get a real pair of fresh ones. Once in awhile an elk does shed both antlers at once, and if it were seen "in the act," such a pair could be obtained. Otherwise, finding dropped antlers of necessary quality is too precarious. Although I had not been able to prove this through consultation with biologists, I thought there might be a difference in the quality and texture of a "live" antler as compared with a "dead" antler. As demonstrated, one of the antlers I found seemed to be of excellent quality. The other looked just as good—even better—but would not stand up under the severe strain of the tension and compression. To my mind, the good one must have been a fresher one, more nearly "alive." But herein lies the difficulty of trying to find proper quality in dropped antlers.

Following this line of reasoning I was delighted to get a pair of antlers from a bull elk that had been kept under special supervision on the refuge. His antlers were shed within minutes of each other, and he seemed to be in excellent condition, but his antlers were the worst of any I had tried so far. After sawing out the strips I boiled them for hours before they became soft enough to bend at all, and then one after the other broke into a dozen pieces as we tried to straighten them out on the form. I decided that the "civilized" diet fed this prize bull had not produced the best-quality antlers.

The "live" antler on the head of the animal may be of even better quality than a freshly dropped antler, I thought. Most elk drop their antlers in March, but some are dropped in late January and some do not fall off until April or even May. So much depends upon the condition of the animal. The rutting season begins in the fall just after the antlers have shed their velvet; so they are in their prime. Shortly thereafter the antlers begin to deteriorate and eventually fall off.

I thought I would make one more try with antlers as nearly alive as it is possible to get them. I acquired a pair of nice ones from a middle-aged bull just shot by a hunter, but they proved to be even worse than those of the prize bull. So now I am not so sure of the "civilized diet," but think perhaps even the natural diet may not be adequate nowadays.

One other thing I should mention. These last two experiments were made with boiling water only. After one limb broke on the little elk horn bow I thought perhaps the Prestone, since it was not pure glycerin, might have contained chemicals that adversely affected the antler. With an extra strip of antler I discovered that boiling water was adequate for bending it. But now I wonder if the Prestone was not better after all. Perhaps water alone absorbed too much of the natural glue from the antler, causing it to become too brittle and break.

I have tried another experiment. It came to mind that in boiling the antlers for such a long time they must lose a lot of gelatin and glue. This might account for some of the failures, although I still have no good idea why some come out well and others do not. Recently I sawed off a slice of antler and soaked it in rain water (really melted snow) to which I added quite a bit of glue made by boiling down a lot of sinew scraps. The amount of glue was enough that the solution felt a bit heavy and sticky but was not enough to cause jelling when it was cold. The piece of antler was soaked in this glue water for a week, then covered and boiled rather hard for three hours. Removing the antler I heated it gently over an electric burner until it was so hot I could barely handle it and clamped it to a form to add a curve like a reflex and also to try to straighten the slice.

Everything worked fine. Bending the curve was easy; the straightening not so easy. In fact it was impossible to straighten out one rather acute bend. I am more convinced than ever that it is impossible to straighten more than the slightest curve in the shank of the antler; so it would also be impossible to make a bow of a single length of antler unless one could be found with a shank that is at least straight in one plane. This slice of antler was from the prize bull from which the two limbs previously tried had failed so miserably. Even with this boiling of only three hours the central porous part of the antler disintegrated, but the horn itself remained in good condition. I am now further encouraged to try another elk horn bow and hope that I can acquire a pair of antlers that will prove of good enough quality to warrant the effort. (Practice makes experience!)

The fact that that one limb on the bow I made survived the terrific strain to which it was submitted makes me want to keep trying. The remaining good limb on that little bow is so beautiful that I hope I shall yet produce a workable, practical elk horn bow. If the sinew itself were allowed to do all the reflexing, the finished forty-inch bow would probably be about thirty-seven or thirty-eight inches across the tips instead of the twenty-nine inches on the bow that broke. This would greatly ease the tension.

Another thing I would like to try: I talked with a biologist who thinks the antler would be most resilient at the time the velvet is shed, either immediately before or immediately after the shedding. At this time the soft immature cartilage is changing over to hard bonelike material, and if we could obtain the antlers before they have acquired their full amount of calcium, we might have the material we are looking for. However, to get such a pair of antlers would seem impossible these days because the hunting season does not open until bulls are in rut, by which time the antlers are completely mature, hard, and bonelike as we are accustomed to seeing them.

Another possibility, just called to our attention by Milford Chandler: could "elk" antler really have been caribou antler? Caribou horn is more dense than elk horn, with a less porous core, or center. The caribou were occasionally seen as far south as the area of the horn bows.

I still think as good or better a bow can be made of wood and sinew, with a lot less work. And I feel the mountain-sheep horn bow is more certain of success and would have been easier to work and to handle for a warrior who felt he had to have a horn bow of some kind for the sake of its medicine or for prestige. Perhaps because the production of the elk horn bow was so precarious it was the more expensive one to buy. Although it may not have been any more efficient than either mountain-sheep horn or one of the better woods, it may have sold for more horses and must have been a prized possession.

Of the many horn bows of every description I have seen in museums, my recollection would be that at least two out of three were definitely mountain sheep. The other third might be elk, or baleen as already stated.

After all I have said about elk horn and baleen, here are a few more considerations. I have never heard that any of the whaling Indians of northern California and the Northwest Coast ever used baleen as bow material, but this does not rule out possibilities of its use by the Plateau and Northern Plains tribes. The seafaring tribes did not depend upon archery to the extent that some of the interior tribes did, although they did have beautiful bows similar to those of other California tribes. They already had the very short, wide bows of juniper and yew and perhaps reserved the baleen for trade. They were great traders, and there were established trade routes all across the country centuries ago.

It may be that my experiments with Jackson's Hole elk horn would not tell the whole story about elk antler. Since the early 1900s this area has had the largest elk herd in the entire United States, but the majority of these magnificent animals were originally to be found east of the continental divide, usually in or close to wooded areas along the great rivers of the West. Our Jackson's Hole elk winter and shed their antlers on the National Elk Refuge, and the high altitude, artificial feeding of hay and nutrient pellets, and the change of environment generally may have a great effect on their condition and well being. These factors could also influence the condition of the antlers. I wonder if the elk of a hundred years ago or more, on their former range, might not have had stronger, more resilient antlers with heavier outer layers and less porous material in the center. Size alone does not always indicate an animal's true physical condition. In nature the smaller varieties are often better than the larger. A big potato may look good but may be hollow inside. A big apple may appear beautiful yet have no flavor.

Our old Kiowa friend Tahan told us the soldiers made fun of his pony, calling it a scrawny little old jack rabbit. On a wager he on his little "jack rabbit" beat the best hot-blooded horses on the post, and his Indian cronies went home with most of the cavalrymen's recent pay issue. The Indian horses had had to be content with willow browse, cottonwood bark, and dry grass all winter but these evidently were more nourishing and produced more vitality than hay and grain did for the army horses. The cavalrymen should have known by then that Indian ponies, men, women, children, and dogs often traveled twice as far in a day as the army could with all its blooded horses.

Environment and nutrition could have had much to do with the quality of the antlers Indians might have used for bows. This is the only explanation I can imagine that could account for the figures on cross sections of bows that possibly were of elk horn.

Occasional mention has been made of bows of buffalo ribs. I heard much about such unusual bows while on the Standing Rock Reservation from my old friend Flying Cloud, but I have never seen a bow that could have been made of this material. I seldom say anything is impossible, but making such a bow would have been even more difficult than making one of antler or horn. Furthermore, with all the good bow woods available to the Sioux I cannot imagine why anyone would want to make a bow of buffalo ribs unless it was for some ceremonial or "medicine" purpose.

The Sioux have stories about the bow coming from the moon, as do the Osages, Pawnees, and perhaps some other tribes. Walking Bull told us one such story about Iktomi, the Spider Man. Iktomi was living with the people at the edge of the camp. He had a small yellow lodge, not very good looking.

One day runners came into camp shouting that a great giant was going through the land eating up all the people. A council was called immediately but no one seemed to know what to do. The chief's beautiful daughter finally came forward and said she would marry the man who killed the giant.

Iktomi spoke right up and said he could do it, but everyone laughed at him and wanted to know what he could do.

"I won't tell you what I can do, but no one else has any ideas so you had better give me a chance," said Iktomi.

So, since it was a last resort, he was told to go ahead.

"All right," said Iktomi, "but you must all do just as I say. First of all I want everyone to bring me his bow and arrows."

So everyone brought his bow and all his arrows. There were some very fine ones, some of horn, beautifully made, but Iktomi would look each one over then throw it down in disgust.

"These are no good," he cried. "Do you mean to tell me you have brought me all the bows and arrows in camp?"

"We brought you everything except the bow and arrows of that little boy who lives with his grandmother. He has never had any one to teach him. All he has is a bent stick with a string on it and a couple of crooked bone-headed arrows."

"Well, then, bring them to me. I told you to bring me *all* the bows and arrows and you are not playing fair," said Iktomi.

So they brought him the little boy's poor bow and poor arrows. The bow looked more like a new moon than a real bow but Iktomi picked it up and cried out, "*Waśte!* [Good!] This is just what I want!" All the people were amazed and made the sign for crazy, turning their fists in a twisting motion in front of their foreheads.

Iktomi started out and by and by he saw a great cloud coming which he thought might be the giant, and he was frightened. "The whole sky is coming after me!" he said to himself. But it proved to be only a magpie flying, and Iktomi was relieved.

The magpie flew up to Iktomi and said, "Brother, a great giant is going through the land and is eating up all the people."

Iktomi told the magpie, "Go and tell the giant that a great person is coming. Tell him I have fought with the moon and am now bringing it with me. Tell him I am looking for him."

Iktomi stamped his foot on the ground and blew, "Hu-uh! Hu-uh!" and blew the magpie right back to the giant.

The magpie said to the giant, "Brother, a great person is coming. He is looking for you. He has fought and conquered the moon and is bringing it with him to fight you!"

So the giant was frightened. Before long Iktomi came over the hill, holding up the toy bow, which looked like the new moon in the evening sky, and singing, *"Ciye, ciye, ciye, wi kiye keyeś kici wecizelo, ciye, ciye!* [Brother, I even fought with the moon and I am going to fight you too!]"

The giant was so frightened that he started to run away, so Iktomi shot him in the back with one of his crooked bone-tipped arrows, and the giant fell over dead.

Then Iktomi went over to him, took out his knife, and cut the giant's stomach open, and all the people came out and went back home, and everyone was happy again.

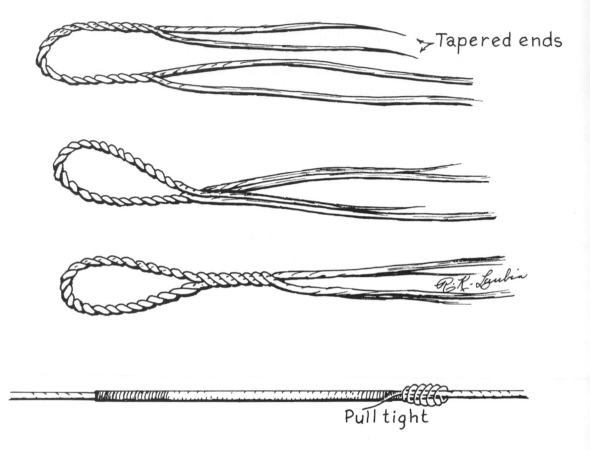

Laying up loops and serving.

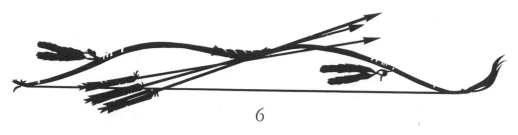

# 6

# *Strings*

Most Plains Indians preferred sinew from the buffalo's loin for bow strings, but sometimes deer or even cattle sinew was used.

Not every man made his own strings, anymore than he made his own bows and arrows. There were men, usually older, "retired" men, who specialized in making strings just as others specialized in making bows or arrows.

In making a sinew string a strand of wet sinew was taken and rolled on the thigh, then one end was folded back over a little peg about half way down the strand and twisted with it. By twisting on the thigh the strand was twisted to the right. In bringing the two pieces thus formed together, each was again twisted in the fingers to the right and pulled to the left over the other one. This formed a two-ply string that would not ravel. By splicing in new pieces from opposite sides the splice was always covered by a full piece, and by twisting first right then pulling the far strand to the left the string would never unwind. When the entire length of cord necessary for a bow had been laid up, it was then stretched on the bow or between two pegs until it dried, first having been rubbed with hot thin glue applied with the fingers.

A noose was formed by passing the single standing end of the cord through the loop formed where the first strand of sinew was bent back when the twisting was begun. It has often been stated that this noose was placed on the lower end of the bow, but this is only partially true. If the bow had only one notch at one end, that is where the noose was placed; however, this often became the upper end of the bow when the bow was in use. To finish stringing the bow, the noose end was placed on the ground under the right instep, or to protect the tip of the bow better, over and against the right foot, while the left hand held the other end of the bow and the bow was bent by pressing its center with the right knee and pulling with the left hand. With the right hand the free end of the bow string was given a turn around the upper end of the bow, which usually contained two notches, then tied in two half hitches. In other words, the bow was strung while upside down. In use the bow was ordinarily held with the noose end up, and in unstringing, the noose was slipped out of the single notch in the same way as when unstringing any other kind of bow.

Apparently there were exceptions in which the tied end remained the upper end. There was no set rule. One man's choice may have been one way, another man's another. Once the string was attached in its right place, the bow was braced from then on in the same manner as most other bows, merely by holding the lower tip under the left foot, pulling the handle of the bow to the left and pushing the noose into place with the right hand. A plain bow, or a bow with a slight reflex, could be strung this way even while on horseback. So it seems that most men carried the bow, after the first stringing, with the noose end, or single-notched end, up. When the bow had a single notch at both ends, the noose end was up, but it was the owner's choice which end received the noose in the first place.*

In stringing a highly reflexed bow, especially one that had no real nocks but only small ridges built up of sinew, the bow had to be restrung each time it was used because the string would not stay on when the bow was relaxed. Some of these reflexed bows were so strong that one man, from a sitting position, bent the bow with both hands over his knee while another put the string in place. Before stringing, such a bow was usually hung in the sun for awhile or gently heated over coals from the fire. Except for some modern bows, mainly to sell to tourists, I have never heard of any Indians who had a permanent loop tied, twisted, or spliced into the bow string. The noose was the nearest thing to it and was used all across the country. The noose slips out of one notch easier than out of two, which is the probable reason for this peculiar type of nock.

My Cheyenne bow and a few bows from other tribes, including the Apaches, has a more complicated tie on the permanent end of the string. The string is first hooked over the tip of the bow at the nock, brought around over

---

*In South America some bows had permanent strings, and some tribes made the back of the bow concave, or even grooved, with a string twice as long as necessary. After stringing the bow the extra string was brought down the back and held in place with several turns around the other tip. If the string broke, this extra length was then used to restring the bow. For more information on South American bows and arrows see Julian H. Steward's *Handbook of South American Indians,* Bureau of American Ethnology *Bulletin* 143, 5:229–44.

itself, then turned back the opposite way, brought around again and tied in two half hitches. On some bows this reverse turn is made under the taut string, on others it is over.

On a Seneca bow in the New York State Museum in Albany the tie is made by going around the bow first above the taut string, again around and under, then it is reversed, pulled back under the last turn, then over and under it, finally ending in a clove hitch. It seems quite a complicated tie and it certainly ought to be secure.

To summarize the materials previously mentioned: strings were made of various kinds of sinew—buffalo, moose, elk, deer. Winnebagoes made strings of snapping turtle neck; Senecas used woodchuck skin; Cherokees used bear gut and possibly also woodchuck. Luiseños are said to have used dogbane, milkweed, or stinging-nettle fibers. Mostly they made two-ply strings, but some were three-ply or even four-ply. When they used sinew, they made a three-ply string of it. Sparkman wrote that they unstrung the bow to save the string, which may be partially true, but the main reason for unstringing any bow is to save the bow.

Some southern Indians made strings of wild hemp, while in the Southwest yucca or agave were occasionally used. However, sinew was probably the easiest material for most tribes to obtain and actually made the best string.

I have made sinew strings many times for my "Indian" bows, but when I shoot I have gone modern in one regard. I usually use dacron for the strings. It is far better than linen, which was formerly used on "white men's" bows, and it is a good substitute for the raw silk of the Turks. Sinew was the best the Indians had, but even a sinew string has to be built up heavier than dacron, which impedes the cast, and it is highly affected by weather. When it rained, the Indians called off a fight. They thought white men foolish to fight in all kinds of weather. White Bull said the white men took all the fun out of fighting.

For the bows I ordinarily use I make a dacron string of about ten threads, with a two-ply twist for loops at both ends. For a forty-eight-inch bow I drive a couple of small nails into a board, setting them about sixty inches apart, attach the thread to one and run it around the two nails five times, thus giving me the amount necessary for the bow string. I wax this well with beeswax, then cut it through at each nail, making two sixty-inch strands of five threads each. I scrape the ends against a board with a sharp knife to taper them so they will lay nicely, place the two strands together, then about eight inches from one end lay up a loop, with an eye about one and a half inches long, by twisting the two ends back into the main strands, twisting to the right and pulling back to the left, as described for a sinew string.

A string for a forty-eight-inch Martin-type bow should be about forty-four inches long, so the other loop can be laid in to correspond to this length. The two strands between the loops—the main bow string itself—need be given only a few twists to keep them together. The final length, when applied to the bow, can be adjusted by twisting or untwisting as much as is necessary. Just the twisting necessary to lay up the loops will use up all the extra length obtained when cutting the thread in the first place.

A string like this should be "served," that is, wound with another thread, preferably carpet thread, after the bow is braced. This should be done for several inches where the fingers hold the arrow on it. Without any mechanical gadgets I can lay up a good string in about half an hour.

So far as I know, Indians did not serve a sinew string, but those who used fiber must have done so because it would not stand much shooting otherwise.

## BRACER

Most Indians used small bracers, or arm-guards of some sort. On the East Coast some were made of wood, others of woven material. Plains Indians made them of rawhide. Eskimos made attractive bracers of walrus ivory. The leather or rawhide bracers were similar to the ones with which we are all familiar, although they were usually smaller.

The Navajo bracer, or *kehto,* was made in recent times of harness leather, with a heavy silver ornament on the outside of the arm. It served as decoration only. The harness leather, which absorbed the shock of the bow string, was lined with a piece of thin leather which served as a pocket or a purse. These are still made sparingly today, although the Navajos gave up archery long ago.

The *kehto* I have was used nearly a century ago in the Navajo-Hopi war. It was given to me by a friend to whom the old Navajo who owned it would not sell the leather guard, as he considered it the most important part. I made a new guard of harness leather and laced it to the silver ornament with sinew as was done on the original.

Recently we read an article which stated that the silver *kehto* of the Navajos was the part of the bracer to take the blow from the string. This is contrary to what we have been told and what we have learned for ourselves. A *kehto* cast out of silver as so many were would fray the string very rapidly,

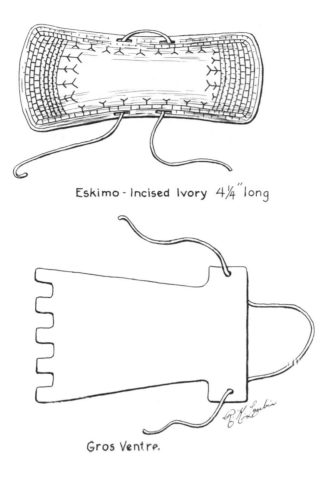

Eskimo - Incised Ivory 4¼" long

Gros Ventre.

Bracers.

and a silver plate with turquoise ornamentation like mine would catch the string. Of course, the Navajos did not learn to set turquoise until about 1880; so before that time, when archery was still in vogue, it would have been possible to make a plain flat silver *kehto*. They learned to do silver work about the middle of the nineteenth century. Nevertheless, we still think the silver was merely ornamental, worn on the *outside* of the arm, and not the inner part of the bracer which was struck by the bow string. The fact that the Navajo warrior who originally wore the bracer I now have would not part with the leather, which he said was the important part, makes us feel that the silver was merely ornamental. If it had some symbolic meaning, the chances are he would not have parted with either the silver or the leather.

When I offered my tackle to Chief One Bull he first picked up the leather bracer I used at that time and immediately tied it on. He knew what it was and must have been accustomed to using one in earlier times.

7

# *Arrows*

If Indian bows generally have a poor reputation, arrows have a still worse one. Complaints are heard that they are not made well, that they are made of poor materials, that they are poorly fletched, that the feathers are too long, that the shafts are too short, that they are badly designed, that the shafts are of odd lengths, and so on.

As with bows there is no single classification of Indian arrows. Differences depend upon the location where they were made, the available materials, and the ideas and skills of local makers. Arrows differ even within the same area and the same tribe.

The motion picture industry has done about as poor a job of depicting Indian archery as it has any other facet of Indian life. The bows are usually some commercial variety that do not look a bit Indian, and so are the arrows. I remember a movie made a number of years ago which portrayed a cattle drive on the western plains. Suddenly an arrow thudded into the wagon seat behind the driver. It was as commercial an arrow as has ever been seen, a typical broadhead, with large parabolic feathers and brilliant cresting. The driver reached around, pulled it out without any difficulty, gave it a cursory examination and pronounced it Comanche. He could just as well have said Sioux, or Cheyenne, or Kwakiutl, for as long as it did not look like any Indian arrow he could have called it anything. Almost the same thing happened in a more recent picture billed, as usual, as an authentic Indian portrayal. The "Crow" arrow supposedly had a stone point, which in hitting a post as this one did would have snapped off completely. The feathers had been left untrimmed apparently to make it look primitive. It not only had cresting like any other arrows one can buy but also had a crest farther down on the shaft. The shaft itself was large enough and long enough for a six-foot-long bow. An old Crow arrow maker would have been mortified.

On the other hand, in museums people see Indian arrows with the feathers half off, the shafts badly warped, and wonder how the Indians ever hit anything with such projectiles. The answer is that they didn't. As with the bows, most of the museum specimens are so old that it is hard to tell now what they once looked like.

There is no doubt that most Indians did not have the arrow materials that are available to archers today, nor the tools and machinery to turn out the perfect shafts that have been on the market for many years. But they knew that an arrow to fly straight must be straight, and did the best they could to make it that way. Being made of natural shoots and having to be treated with heat and straighteners to make them serviceable, such arrows eventually warped badly. Arrows that were kept on hand for any length of time were periodically put through a straightening process. Those we see in the museums have not been so fortunate.

The Sioux made arrows from shoots of plum, cherry, and osier (so-called red willow, really a dogwood), but preferred serviceberry and wild currant. These woods are hard but flexible, and if an animal rolls over on one it drives in farther or merely bends instead of breaking off. Other tribes used the same kinds when available. The shoots were gathered as straight as possible, cut when the sap was down in the late fall or late winter, just before it started up again, wound with thongs, and tied tightly in bundles and dried, usually being hung up high to a lodge pole for several weeks.

When making the shoots up into arrows each was scraped to remove the bark, greased, heated over coals raked out of the fire, and straightened holding it in the teeth and working with both hands. Sometimes the help of a straightener of horn, bone, antler, or stone, which served as a kind of wrench, was needed. Finally each shaft was sized, smoothed, and polished with a pair of sandstone blocks about six inches long, each block being grooved down its length to the size the arrow was to be made. The shaft was placed between the grooves and worked back and forth.

I have Sioux arrows made by eight different men. The shafts for each set are the same but vary from other sets, being from 22 1/2 to 25 inches long, with the average being about 23 inches. Feathers run from 5 1/2 to 7 1/2 inches. Most shafts are about 5/16 inch in diameter, but one set is 3/8 inch. Some of these arrows are still straight, but many are now warped from laying idle so many years. Most of these Sioux arrows have iron points, and most have turkey feathers, but Philip Returns-from-Scout made me some arrows with bone points and with hawk feathers dyed blue and yellow. He wanted me to see the kind of arrows his father used, although he did not groove them. He said that all Sioux arrows were grooved in early days. Originally the Sioux did not use turkey feathers on their arrows because there were few or no turkeys in their area. They used hawk or eagle or some other bird of prey that was a great hunter and that would ascribe such power to the arrows. However, one old man said he always used one pelican feather on his arrows; the other two were from some other kind of bird. In his case the pelican was probably some special "medicine."

Old Sioux warriors I knew insisted that the grooves in the shaft represented lightning and made the arrow fly straight. In fact, some insisted an arrow would not fly straight unless so treated. Some of us have heard the remark that lightning never strikes twice in the same place (a false supposition), which would hardly induce accuracy, but the speed and destruction of the lightning is what the Indian warriors had in mind. They also said that the grooves kept the shaft from warping, and it may have had some deterrent effect. I make my arrows Indian-style but of Port Orford cedar, and I groove them just to make them look more Indian. I have lost arrows in the fall and found them the following summer. After laying under the snow and being in the wet all that time they have still been straight. I have lost commercially made arrows in the same way and found them badly warped. Maybe it was just coincidence. But no arrow artificially straightened in the first place, as the Indians had to do, will stay straight forever, although the grooves may have delayed warping.

It is certain that the grooves had nothing to do with bleeding an animal, and it would seem that they were mainly ceremonial. All the Plains tribes, the Plateau tribes who sometimes frequented the plains, and the Apaches grooved their arrows when using wooden shafts. Apache arrows I have seen had only two grooves, however. Northwest Coast Indians and Eskimos did not; and the cane and reed shafts were not grooved.

Several authors have criticized Indian arrows for their long feathers, stating that they contribute nothing whatever to accuracy and actually impede the flight. I must take issue with such a statement, as I have with many others. My reason is that I have gained much of my knowledge of Indian archery by actual experience coupled with explanations given to me by older Indians. Tests I have carried out convince me that the long feathers definitely stabilize the arrow's flight. A well-made Indian arrow will fly every bit as well as a commercial arrow. I have tested Indian-style arrows against modern hunting and roving arrows and found they outshot them both. They are just as accurate and shoot farther from the same bow. The modern hunting and roving arrows may have somewhat shorter feathers, but they are higher. The Indian arrows have the feathers trimmed down so low that they offer less air resistance.

There were tribal styles of arrows but often with such slight differences that it would be difficult or impossible to name the tribe from which an isolated arrow came. The nocks were often the most distinctive parts of the arrows, but even this is no sure test to determine the tribe. Of the eight Sioux arrow makers I mentioned, four cut their notches so nearly alike as to be almost indistinguishable. The other four are quite different, bringing the nocks to a point, rounding them off, or leaving them flat. All of them used a U-shaped notch about 1/8 inch wide and 3/16 inch deep in a bulbous nock, some more bulbous than others.

It is perfectly possible to shoot these arrows with the Mediterranean release, even though the Sioux release employs all four fingers and the thumb. The slight swell at the nock makes for quicker taking from the quiver, easier placement on the string, and better hold.

I have two arrows from the Southern Plains, which may be either Kiowa or Comanche. They were picked up after a battle in Indian Territory. The nocks are wide, flaring, V-shaped rather than bulbous. The iron points are shorter than Sioux points, 1 5/8 inches long instead of 2 3/4 or 3 inches. Feathers on one are 4 1/2 inches long, 5 1/2 inches on the other. The shaft with the shorter feathers is 9/32 inch thick and 23 3/4 inches long, the other 11/32 inch thick and 24 1/4 inches long. These Southern Plains arrows have three grooves each, almost perfectly straight.

The arrows made for me by Mouse's Road, the Cheyenne, have nocks like some of my Sioux arrows, but the fletching is quite different, and the shafts are crested with a series of red rings outlined with black—evidently the old man's way of holding to the Cheyenne tradition as the "Striped Arrow People."

A Sioux warrior or hunter measured his arrows this way: he took the measurement from his elbow to the tip of his middle finger and added the distance from his wrist to the big knuckle of the middle finger. Omahas also measured arrows like that. A man of any prestige had what we might call a professional arrow maker make arrows to his specifications, and he usually ordered a hundred at a time. (A high-ranking warrior might give as much as a horse for ten good arrows.) Even so, he often kept arrow stock on hand in his own tipi, and in an emergency could either make arrows himself or turn the seasoned shafts over to the arrow maker for immediate manufacture. Extra arrows were stored in a rather rough, undecorated quiver until those in his utility quiver needed replacement.

After the shafts were cut to length and completely straightened, the Sioux arrow maker prepared the nocks. The heavy, or butt, end of the shaft was always used for the nock. Thus the arrow traveled in the direction the shoot was growing. The shaft itself was trimmed thinner just below the nock and nicely tapered toward the point, so that the finished arrow was slightly barreled. The notch itself was cut in with a sharp knife, sometimes even with a round file obtained from the traders. Originally they must have been cut in, or sawed in, with a stone tool. In the later days of Plains Indian archery a saw was made from a table knife with the teeth filed in. Such a saw was used to cut the slot in the point of the arrow for inserting the arrowhead.

Next came the grooving. Sometimes the graver used was merely a very sharp iron or steel arrowhead, held vertically to the shaft. The usual Sioux grooving started with a straight line at a point near where the feathering was to begin and, after an inch or so, became wavy or zigzagged towards the head of the arrow. Within about three inches of the head it became straight again. I have seen a few Sioux arrows with either straight lines or slightly wavy lines all the way, and some with quite angular zigzags. Three grooves were so cut, paralleling each other as nearly as it was possible for the engraver to do by eye.

Long ago I was informed that there was another form of graver sometimes used. It consisted of a piece of bone through which a hole was drilled somewhat smaller than the diameter of the arrow. A projecting point, or spur, was then cut and the remainder of the hole enlarged to the size of the finished arrow. This little point served as the graving tool. The arrow was pulled through the hole, and the sharp point cut the groove. In more recent times some Indians actually obtained graving tools, or made them from nails by setting a nail in a handle and grinding off the tip to approximate a true graver. They must have considered the grooves important to go to all the trouble involved in cutting them.

After the grooves were cut in, the shaft was again polished, using fine sandstone, and lastly was rubbed with a piece of heavy buckskin, or even with grass.

Iron and even steel arrowheads were procured from the white traders, but

Indians often cut them from thin iron frying pans and also from wagon hoops. Lewis and Clark sold pieces of sheet iron four inches square to some of the Village Indians for seven or eight gallons of corn each.

As a rule there was no difference in the shape of war or hunting points when made of metal, although occasional examples of barbed metal war arrowheads have been noted. Flint or jasper war points were often triangular, being loosely set in the shaft with little or no binding so that the head remained in the wound on withdrawing the shaft.

There are stories that war points were set on the arrows so as to be perpendicular to the bowstring; the idea was that the arrowhead would then enter a man's ribs more easily. Conversely, hunting points were set in the same line as the string to enter an animal's rib cage more readily. If the Indians ever had such ideas they were impractical because any arrow, no matter how it is fletched, will spin while traveling, and no one can predict at what angle it will arrive in its target. The arrows I own have points set every which way. Some are at an angle, which, when you consider that the bow itself was always held on an angle, would mean that the points would be horizontal when they left the bow. But this still does not mean that they would be horizontal when they reached the target. Actually the point set in this way, crosswise to the string, gives some advantage, as it permits a longer draw on the arrow.

The metal points were usually set in warm glue, then wrapped tightly with wet sinew. Deer loin sinew was preferred for this. As the sinew dries it shrinks, so that it holds the point very tightly. The finished wrapping lays so tight, smooth, and flat as to be almost part of the shaft, far superior to even the finest of silk thread.

The cresting was added before the feathers were attached. Usually the colors were in the form of a dye, rather than a paint, and water colors were used in recent years. Just as modern arrows are crested, the bands of color were applied on the shaft to come between the feathers. Every man had his own cresting, and sometimes arrows were further distinguished with teeth marks, nicks, or scratches. In this way there were never any arguments as to whom a game animal belonged. The arrow in the carcass was proof enough who was the owner of the meat. The most typical colors used were red and black, but I have some arrows crested with blue, green, and yellow. Sometimes even the sinew wrappings were colored.

Feathers were split with a sharp knife, then carefully scraped to remove excess pith and to make the midrib as thin as possible; one end of the feather was held in the teeth while the scraping was done. They were also trimmed with a knife or, when available, with scissors, which made the job much easier. The Sioux arrow maker, after carefully applying hot glue to the scraped midrib, placing the feathers, and holding them with his left-hand fingers, started a sinew wrapping with his right hand. Any strand of sinew is slightly heavier at one end than the other; the thin end of properly prepared sinew tapers out to a fine point. The sinew was soaked in water to which a little glue had been added. The fletcher started wrapping with the heavy end, then held the thin end in his teeth and finished the wrapping by turning the shaft with his fingers, carefully terminating with the thin pointed end.

The feathers were set about an inch below the nock. Not all feathers were glued, but the best arrows had the feathers glued as well as wrapped. After the wrapping was complete a glue stick (described in Chapter 8) was moistened and applied to both arrowhead and feather wrappings. Then the glue was rubbed down with the thumb nail, or with a little shell attached by a thong to the thumb. The feathers so wrapped offered no sharp edges or points to the hand as is so often the case with glued-on feathers on modern arrows when no arrow rest is used on the bow. Sometimes a long wisp of web was left on each feather at its forward end for decoration, and at other times a bit of colored down was wrapped under the sinew, also for decoration.

Generally the Sioux used three feathers on an arrow, but occasionally only two were used. The arrows Philip Returns-from-Scout made for me have very slightly spiraled feathers, but all my other Sioux arrows have the feathers laid on parallel to the shaft. The only spiraling is due to the natural curve of the feathers. Even this is enough that the arrows spin in flight.

The final touch to an arrow to be used for hunting buffalo was to cere- monially smear it with buffalo blood.

The Luiseño Indians of Southern California, one of the Shoshonean groups, evidently spiraled the feathers on their arrows. Philip Sparkman wrote: "Three trimmed feathers are attached to the shaft by wrapping with sinew, a little asphaltum being used to keep the sinew threads from slipping out of place. The feathers are not tied straight to the shaft, but twisted slightly to one side, the object being to give a rotary motion to the arrow and so, it is thought, hold it straighter in its course, on the same principle as the spiral grooving of a rifle barrel. The feathers used are mainly from different species of hawks."[1]

The real purpose of the asphaltum must have been to waterproof the bind- ing, as the sinew will not slip when applied with glue, as has been described for other tribes.

Sparkman also said Luiseño bows would shoot about one hundred yards and were efficient at half that distance, but says little else about them.

Lewis and Clark said that the Shoshonis (of Idaho) made arrows similar to those of other tribes but that they were more slender.

I remember long ago hearing someone quote an old Indian, "Any stick make-um bow. Arrow him heap much work."

I once asked One Bull and some other old-timers if they ever made stone arrowheads. The reply was no. One Bull told me that at Arrowhead Butte, in South Dakota, they used to find many stone arrowheads that must have been cached there long ago by people formerly living in the area. They used them when they found them, but when I asked who made them he replied, "Iktomi made them." Later he elaborated and said the Little Iktomi, or Little Spider People, made them. Flying Cloud told us a story about a man named Crooked Neck who heard a little clicking noise one day and looked around to find its source. He found some Little Spider men making arrowheads. He watched them for awhile, then decided he would take some of the arrowheads for his own use. But when he picked up a couple of them, one of the Little Iktomi took a tiny bow and an arrow and shot him in the neck. From that time on he always had a wry neck, and the people called him Crooked Neck.

I have also asked old men of Crow, Cheyenne, and Blackfoot tribes about arrowheads, and all told me the same thing: Old Man Coyote, Wihio, Napi— the legendary culture heroes, or tricksters—made them.

No doubt all these tribes who now have no tradition of making stone arrowheads once made them, but after moving out onto the prairies the proper stone for making them was scarce or nonexistent. Bone was much easier to obtain and served as well for their type of hunting. The bone used was usually from the foreleg of an elk between the fetlock and knee joint, but sometimes ribs were used. In fact any bone that would yield a flat piece for the arrowhead could be used. Actually it was more difficult to make a bone point than it was to chip a stone one, but after obtaining saws and files the task was much easier. The arrows Philip Returns-from-Scout made for me all had points of different shapes, all beautifully made.

Today there are more white men who know how to make stone arrowheads than there are Indians who can do it. In the eastern part of the country the making of stone implements disappeared within the first hundred years of white contact. Some Cherokee craftsmen have recently revived the art of stone chipping, having learned it from a white hobbyist. The last North American Indian to make stone points for practical purposes was probably Ishi, whom we have mentioned before. While he was at the museum of the University of

California he made beautiful little points of glass from various colored bottles. Points from old beer bottles look like obsidian and can hardly be distinguished from it. Ishi also used milk glass, red, blue, amber, and green glass. Some of his arrows were foreshafted cane; each foreshaft had one of these pretty little glass points.

A good modern arrowhead maker can turn out a very good and serviceable point of glass or obsidian in as few as twenty minutes. Obsidian points have been found to have better penetration on game than those of the finest steel. It takes me at least an hour to make a nice bone point, and while it is pretty and could be useful, it would not be as good as an obsidian point. But Plains Indians had little other choice. They did, however, make points from the heavy cartilage in a buffalo's neck and from the tendons in the leg. When shaped and dried these were very serviceable; the Indians claimed they would bend around a bone without breaking as happened with a stone or bone point when it struck a bone. Piercing a bone, as sometimes happened with metal arrowheads, inflicted little damage either.

The Sioux made blunt arrows with heavy conical or bulbous heads for killing birds and small game. These were usually boys' arrows. Some were fletched, often with only two feathers, others had bare shafts, and none of these blunts I have seen was grooved.

The Sioux did not use poisoned arrows, and there is little evidence that any Plains tribes did. Some tribes in other parts of the country did use snake venom or poison of one type or another on their arrows, although no North American Indians made a vegetable poison such as was used by some South American tribes.

## OTHER ARROWS

All sorts of materials were used for arrowheads, depending upon the locality. I once found an arrowhead of deer bone at an old village site in Connecticut. It is merely a toe bone, the tip becoming the point, and the other end drilled deep enough to fit a shaft into it. The shaft could have been held in place with a little pitch or glue. Similar points have been reported for many areas; some were made from the tips of antler prongs.

I also found a black jasper "turtleback" point at old Fort Amanda, Ohio. At that time I supposed it had been used in a battle against soldiers stationed at the fort, but there was never a battle there. The fort had merely been garrisoned during the War of 1812 as a precaution against Indian raids. That arrowhead must have been laying there for a long time before I came along, and it would be interesting to know its history, because there is no black jasper in Ohio. Obsidian points have also been found on occasion in many parts of the country, although obsidian is found only in certain Rocky Mountain areas. There were trade routes up and down and across the country long before Columbus arrived, and one of the important articles of trade was good arrow-point material.

Some people think the now well-known Folsom points were arrow points but they are dated so far back that they must have been used as points on the darts thrown from atlatls, as the bow was unknown in America that long ago.

Ceremonial use may explain some of the beautiful little arrowheads, often called "gem points," that have been found in some parts of the country. Certainly they had no practical value. They may even have been made as tests of a chipper's skill. Although these little points are also known as "bird points," there is no reason to go to all the work necessary for making such points for killing birds, and they certainly would be of little or no value in killing larger game. A blunt point would do a better job on birds.

Some of the prettiest arrows I have ever seen were made not too long ago by a Caddo named Harry Smith. The nocks are a little less flared than those on some older Caddo arrows, and the feathers are much shorter and trimmed wider than on most Indian arrows. The shafts are of dogwood, 1/2 inch thick and 27 1/2 inches long. With this as a beginning, points 7 1/4 inches long were carved at the heavy, or root, end of the shafts, and the remainder, for its drawing length of 20 1/2 inches, was trimmed to approximately 5/16 of an inch. This entailed a good deal of whittling and shaping but the work is beautifully done, and the shafts are as true as if made from the best dowels. (With most tribes the root end was used for the nock.)

The fletching is with white turkey feathers dyed blue, about 3 5/8 inches long. Some have dark blue cock feathers and light blue hen feathers, and some are the reverse, with light blue cock feathers and dark blue hen feathers. The fletching is further decorated with a bit of webbing from a yellow feather lashed in when the sinew was applied. The points are also decorated with incised diagonal lines, which were filled with red paint. Altogether, these arrows are almost too beautiful to think of shooting them, but old Caddo men insist that such whittled wooden points were common for hunting in earlier days.

The Omahas made some arrows from dogwood shoots, and others were split from a block of ash. Owl feathers were preferred for fletching. Even in recent times fletchers have discovered that owl feathers make the best flight arrows, for they are so light and yet durable. Indians believed the owl feathers helped the arrow to find its mark silently, as the owl flies, and accurately, as the owl catches its prey at night. However, in many tribes owls were taboo except to certain medicine men or other people with power.

Osages, like their relatives the Omahas and the Sioux, often crested arrows with red and black, red for the day, black for the night, as a symbol of precision. In three of their rituals they used two arrows, one black and one red, shot from a bow painted red and black, shooting them towards the setting sun, representing the endless recurrence of night and day. The ritual also represented individual life recurring through descendants. The Omahas used seven arrows in an annual ceremony representing the seven principal gentes of the tribe.[2]

One of the two most important tribal medicines of the Cheyennes is the *Mahuts,* the Sacred Arrows. These four special arrows were believed to have been given to the tribe by the legendary teacher Sweet Medicine, who had received them from Maheo, the Creator. They were taken from the Cheyenne Arrow Keeper by the Pawnees in a battle about 1830. Later the Cheyennes recovered two of them, but the other two have never been returned; so the Cheyennes made two substitutes. These Sacred Arrows are also painted red and black. They have been kept by the Southern Cheyennes most of the time, but in 1957 were brought to the Northern Cheyennes for a special ceremony. The arrows represent the male power of the tribe. They unite the people with the Creator, completing the contact with, and representing the power of, the Supreme Being.[3]

When a boy was born among the Yuchis, a tribe once living in the South east and long associated with the Creeks (both now live in Oklahoma), the father made a tiny bow about eight inches long strung with sinew and four small unfeathered arrows, which he tied to the bow with the umbilical cord. This object was then thrown in the heavy brush where no one could find it and served as a prayer and invocation that the boy would grow to become a master of the weapon in hunting and in war.[4]

In regions where cane and durable reeds were abundant they were used for arrow shafts. The cane of the Southeast is hard enough that the notch for the nock can be cut directly into it and a point of stone, bone, horn, shark tooth, or other suitable material could be set in the shaft proper. In some areas, however, the cane or reed is more fragile; so the nock had to be reinforced with a sinew wrapping, and a hardwood foreshaft was inserted in the forward end. Sometimes this foreshaft, often three-sided and sharp on the point, was all that was used for an arrowhead (see drawing). But at other times an arrowhead was inserted in the tip of the foreshaft and fastened there with sinew. Such arrows were found among the Apaches, the desert tribes, all through California, and up into Oregon, Washington, and British Columbia.

Foreshafts were from 6 to 12 inches long, with the main shaft usually around 25 inches. Most Apache arrows had the parallel nocks and deep notches found on all arrows that are to be used with the Mediterranean release, but a few had the flared, swallow-tailed nocks common to the Southern Plains and Pueblos, which shows that they must have also used a secondary or tertiary release. The shafts are about 11/32 of an inch at the forward end and 5/16 at the nock, showing they did not point the arrow in the direction the cane grew, as was customary with arrows made of shoots. The nock was cut in a joint of the cane. The joints on the shaft were filed smooth. Even some recent Apache arrows had stone tips on the hardwood foreshafts.

Captain Bourke cited a certain Domenech who related "that the Indians have trials of skill with arrows and will often keep ten in the air at one time." Bourke also wrote, "Constant practice had made the Apache dextrous in the use of the bow, arrow and lance; their aim is excellent, and the range attained was perhaps as much as 150 yards."[5]

The Cherokees made a long cane arrow with a shaft as much as thirty-one inches long, which I am sure they did not draw to the head. They used a peculiar fletching, as did their northern relatives the Iroquois (see drawing). The fletching is about six inches long and consists of the tip ends of two turkey feathers, each being left complete for about two and a half inches, then split off the rest of the way. The feather is first laid on the shaft the opposite way, wrapped down at the tip, over the webbing with sinew at the nock, then doubled back to take the usual position on the shaft. The split part of the midrib is glued to the shaft and the forward end, from which the webbing has been peeled, is lashed down with sinew. The arrow is thus fletched with two feathers, but the uncut tips make a distinctive appearance quite different from the usual two-feathered arrow. I have tried such arrows at short distances and found them to fly true, but I imagine they might "plane" on longer flights. It is remarkable that some Cherokees still know about this ancient method of fletching.

Natchez made arrows of reeds tipped with scales of "the armed fish," according to Du Pratz.

Indians on Vancouver Island, in contrast to the long arrows we have been talking about, made arrows only about twenty inches long of pine or cedar, but sometimes they had tips of bone as much as six inches long.

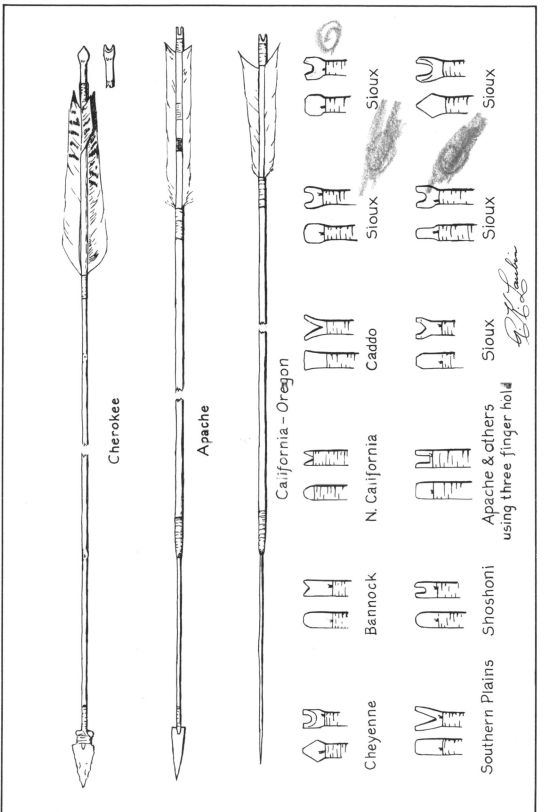

Cherokee

Apache

California – Oregon

Cheyenne

Southern Plains

Bannock

Shoshoni

N. California

Apache & others
using three finger hold

Caddo

Sioux

Sioux

Sioux

Sioux

Sioux

Sioux

Various arrow nocks.

F. H. Cushing, reporting on Zuñi arrows, gave almost the same procedure as just related for the Sioux, and most tribes made arrows in a similar fashion. In addition to the sandstone polishers, the Zuñis also had grooved soapstone blocks, which were heated and the arrow placed between them when too stubborn to be straightened any other way. Similar heating stones have also been reported for the Sioux and other Plains tribes. Zuñi shafts were cut with ceremonies to the wood spirits (as were those of other tribes) and were carried with their upper ends foremost, then passed over the arrowheads, so that they would become acquainted with each other. Shafts to be used for hunting arrows and other peaceful uses were laid with their points to the east or south. Shafts to be used for war were laid with their points to the west or north. They were even peeled from butt to tip, never the other way around, and scraped and shaved butt to tip. They were placed by a hot fire or buried in hot sand to "ripen," and difficult crooked places were straightened with the teeth. The butt end, of course, was the one that received the notch, which was sawed with a flint chip, with the grain, then rasped out with a blunter flint, or with sand and a string. Then the nocks were heated, and the flanges were spread with a heated tool made from a rib, or from stone. If there was any sign of the nock splitting, it was lashed with sinew in addition to the sinew used to bind the feathers.

Zuñi arrows were also grooved. The graver for war arrows was made from a puma or cougar tusk; for peaceful arrows, of elk antler or beaver tooth. The forward ends of the feathers were lashed in place first, and the sinew was held in the teeth, as it was with the Sioux. The grooves also represented lightning striking, as they seemed to do with most, if not all, tribes that used them.[6]

Other Pueblo tribes, as well as the Apaches and Navajos, grooved their arrows when using wooden shafts. Most of the arrows from the desert, California, and the Northwest Coast would be hard to distinguish from arrows of the Plains tribes except those that are made of cane, which the latter did not have.

Coronado reported bone arrowheads for the Pueblo tribes.

Indians always retrieved their arrows whenever possible, because too much work was involved to shoot them away carelessly. In the stories of ancient battles enemy arrows were often returned with a vengeance; it was especially hoped that they might inflict death or injury on their original owners.

In looking at old pictures of the Indian wars one often sees illustrations of bodies of white men full of arrows. Such arrows were shot into the prone dead bodies by warriors riding by at a full gallop. Each warrior might waste

George Catlin's portrait of Tenkswatawa, the "Shawnee Prophet," Tecumseh's brother. Notice the arrows as earrings. Courtesy of the Smithsonian Institution, Bureau of American Ethnology.

some arrows in this way, but the final insult to a hated enemy and challenge to those who might follow were worth the sacrifice of a few arrows.

Certainly Indian arrows were a far cry from the aluminum and fiberglass arrows used today, but for anyone with a feeling for woodcraft and a love of nature, these unnatural materials are cold and without charm. A well-made Indian arrow is a thing of beauty and accurate enough for all but the contest or professional archer who must refine his score with matched arrows to bring it as near to perfection as possible.

# 8

# Quivers

Wherever you find bows and arrows you will also find some kind of case for the arrows, and often for the bow. On the East Coast quivers were made of a sort of basketry or of rushes, sometimes with pretty colors woven into attractive designs. Quivers were often as much as a yard long according to early accounts, and two hands wide at the mouth and one hand at the base. They must have held very long arrows, as has been mentioned for the Cherokees and Iroquois.

Some old drawings show quivers carried at the waist and some on either shoulder, but usually over the right shoulder. I would wager that, unless the archer was left-handed (and, of course, there were some left-handed Indians), it was worn over the left shoulder in traveling. At least, almost all the quivers I have seen of the Plains type were carried so, and all the demonstrations I have had from old Indians would lead me to believe this. Although there are great differences in Indian cultures and traditions, they are generally more like each other than like anything coming out of Europe.

The English tradition is to wear the quiver over the right shoulder, and this is the tradition that modern archers carry on to this day. To me it is a clumsy arrangement, especially with the long arrows most people prefer. Plains quivers, carried over the left shoulder, could be quickly pulled around to the front so that the arrows either projected under the left arm, or they were pulled around still farther so that the quiver sling hung on the back of the neck and the arrows were at the waist with their nocks on the *right*-hand side, where they could be quickly reached while riding. Either way is far more convenient than the English method.

Plains quivers had a bow case attached, and both were attached to a long sling. Consequently I prefer to call the entire arrangement the quiver and separate it into arrow case and bow case. To take up the slack in the long sling, or carrying strap, it was usually placed across the chest and around both shoulders while traveling. A similar long strap was attached to the shield that most warriors carried.

You may be interested in how the warrior put on his shield and quiver. Little Soldier first, and later other old-timers, showed me how they did it. They first laid the quiver on the ground and stepped into it, as they also did immediately following with the shield. This rather strange way of getting into a quiver and shield may have arisen because most warriors of any importance wore eagle feathers or some kind of a headdress, and this really simplified matters. With the shield on top of the quiver it was possible to use it for fending enemy arrows, lance thrusts, or war-club blows, or it could be slid around to the rear to protect the back, or hung over the arm to protect the front. At the same time the warrior could hold his bow arm under it and draw arrows from the quiver with his free hand.

When the warrior was actually in battle, the quiver and empty bow case were practically in his lap, and sometimes he belted them there to ensure that the arrows did not spill out from the jouncing of the horse. In traveling, however, the bow was in its case, attached to the arrow case, and the whole thing hung across his back, suspended as mentioned, with the strap across his chest and with the feathered ends of the arrows pointing to the *left.* This is a little detail that few artists have observed correctly. Knowing only the English style, the majority of artists picture the Indian quiver backward—or else they always draw left-handed Indians!

While riding, the shield was usually hung from the forehorn of the saddle. (Most Indian saddles have a horn fore and aft, rather than the usual cantle.) It may seem a bit awkward for the warrior to have to dismount again in order to step into his shield, but whenever possible he made preparations long in advance of any engagement. War was more of a game than a business; so when the enemy was sighted, time out was taken to put on all warrior clothing and decorations to which a man was entitled—to paint his face, sing his medicine song, and otherwise make ready for an important "show," a spectacular pageant.

Plains Indian quivers were made of buckskin, buffalo hide, otter skin, more recently of cowhide, and most prized by some, cougar, or mountain-lion skin. Most of them had a rawhide disc sewn or laced at the bottom of the arrow case. All except the buckskin quivers had the hair left on as a protection against rain and dampness. A lion-skin quiver used the feet and tail as decorations— one foot at each end of the bow case and one foot on each end of the long carrying strap. The tail made a long pendant below the mouth of the quiver. It was not used as a bow case, as someone once wrote. It would take a giant cougar to have a tail wide enough for even a child's bow.

Most buckskin quivers were elaborately decorated with porcupine quills or beadwork; so they were more for parade than practical use. But even otter-skin and lion-skin quivers and bow cases were usually decorated with beadwork and red flannel. Otter-skin quivers of the Crows and Nez Perces were particularly beautiful. An old Navajo quiver of lion skin has the hair on the outside of the arrow case, but the bow case has the hair inside.

As well as being beautiful the quiver was also very practical. The arrow case, or quiver proper, was usually long enough to nearly cover the arrows. But inside a properly equipped quiver was a "cup" of rawhide, attached to a long stick, into which the arrows were set. So even though the arrows projected only an inch or two, if a man wanted to expose more of them, or wanted to choose a certain arrow, he pulled on the stick, which raised the arrows to the desired height. The projecting end of the stick was also decorated with beads or quills and sometimes with a wisp of horse hair. In the cup he also carried extra arrowheads and a "glue stick," which could be used for repairing arrows. The glue stick was just any little stick six or seven inches long, and it had a ball of hard glue at one end. It could be moistened with the tongue or with water and applied to the sinew of an arrow or arrowhead to aid in binding it to the shaft. Attached to the outside of the quiver was usually a little decorated bag or pouch in which a flint-and-steel fire-making set was carried. These little bags were called "strike-a-light" bags.

Tribes that still used stone arrowheads, as some in California did, placed moss in the bottom of the quiver to protect them from breakage. Most Plains Indians have not used stone points since they left the Woodlands over two hundred years ago, but they did often carry extra tinder of crushed cottonwood or cedar bark in the arrow case, which served to protect the arrow heads and to keep them sharp.

On some quivers even little ornamental dangles of bone or dew claws were attached. When riding horseback an Indian hunter did not worry about the little bit of noise they made. An extra bow string or two were usually tied to the quiver, and sometimes an awl.

I have met some modern bow hunters who say they could never carry an Indian-style quiver because it would make too much noise. The arrows rattle in it. They have all kinds of devices to separate their arrows in a horrible-looking polished leather quiver to keep them from rattling. I doubt that there is one of them who could stalk so quietly that you could hear any noise from his quiver above the noise of his footsteps!

Old Sioux warriors told me that a hunting quiver usually carried ten arrows, but they carried forty arrows when going to war.

Some of the Indians of British Columbia made quivers of wolverine skin. They were made wide enough at the mouth to include the bow while traveling. California Indians made similar quivers of otter skin, deer skin, and even coyote skin. The deerskin quiver was sometimes made from the head and neck of the deer, with the nose as the bottom of the quiver. The Luiseños used fox and wildcat skins for theirs. The quivers of the coastal Indians, in an area of great rainfall, where bows and arrows were often carried in canoes, opened at the side instead of at the top in order to give them more protection from the water. Eskimos made the same kind of quivers from seal or walrus skin.

It is possible that the bow case attached to the Plains quiver is a rather recent addition, developed as a further accommodation to traveling on horseback. An old Crow quiver sketched by Bodmer in 1833 is wide enough at the mouth to contain two short bows as well as the arrows. Catlin during the same period pictured several quivers of various Plains tribes, and although they also have the decorative long flaps at their mouths shown by Bodmer, they have no bow cases. He also shows some quivers that do contain attached bow cases; so this may be about the time when the combined quiver and bow case was developed.

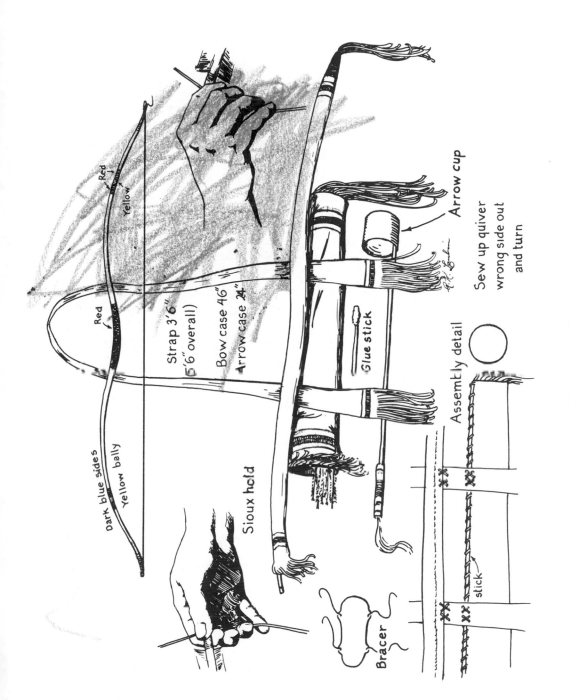

Red

Yellow

Red

Strap 3′6″
(5′6″ overall)

Bow case 46″
Arrow case 24″

Dark blue sides
Yellow belly

Sioux hold

Glue stick

Arrow cup

Sew up quiver
wrong side out
and turn

Assembly detail

stick

Bracer

Quiver assembly.

Ishi shooting Yahi-style. Courtesy of the Lowie Museum of Anthropology, University of California.

# 9

# *Shooting*

Some mention has been made of the Sioux style of shooting. Other Plains Indians shot in similar fashion. They probably developed this style from shooting on horseback, but also used it from a stance. There is no doubt, however, that using a bow in this fashion enables one to handle a heavy bow with more ease than does the usual method of holding it towards the target and drawing the arrow in line with it. The old Indians I knew insisted that the bow must be pushed away at the same time the arrow is drawn towards oneself. Holding the bow overhead before the shot helps accomplish this.

The illustrations show the usual Sioux release, which employs all four fingers and the thumb. It is a very powerful release. Draw, or hold, would be a better term. Mouse's Road, the Cheyenne, used an augmented pinch grip, thumb and forefinger on the arrow and the next two fingers on the string, which is also a strong hold. The so-called Mediterranean release of three fingers, used by most archers today, was used by Eskimos, Indians of southern California and some desert areas, as well as by some of the Apaches. Indians of central California used the Mongolian, or thumb, release, and according to Ernest Thompson Seton, it was also used by the Penobscots of Maine. It seems rather odd that this release should be found only on opposite sides of the continent, but it apparently was unknown to the tribes in between.

In the accounts available about Ishi's shooting, he held the bow at an angle across his body; the upper end was tipped to the left; the arrow was on the right side of the bow, placed so as to lie between his thumb and first finger; the nock of the arrow was held by pressure between the thumb, which drew the string, and the tip of the first finger; the back of the hand was up. All archers using the Mongolian release place the arrow on the right side of the bow. All the other releases place the arrow on the left side of the bow. Naturally we are talking about right-handed archers. It has been stated by some that Indians held the arrow in place with the forefinger of the left hand. The only time this ever happened was when carrying the arrow nocked, all ready to shoot on an instant's notice. But when that time came, the finger was raised or withdrawn to come under the arrow in order not to impede its flight or injure the finger. It has also been stated by the uninformed, or misinformed, that Indians sometimes shot from the right side of the bow. I have already mentioned that this was done only by those using the thumb, or Mongolian, release. It is impossible to do good shooting from the right side of the bow with any other release. One Bull, Kills Pretty Enemy, Tahan, and Mouse's Road laid the arrow over the knuckles of the left hand, on the left side of the bow, just as most other archers do.

Several arrows were usually held in the bow hand, for rapid shooting. It comes as a surprise to most people that these arrows were invariably held points *up.* In the dozens of photographs I have examined of Indians holding bows and arrows in their hands I have found only two with arrow points down. One of these is a photograph of the Osage chief Bacon Rind. The other was of a Yanktonai Sioux. The only reason I know of for pointing the arrows up rather than down is that the arrows are supposed to fly upward and not downward. As far as efficiency goes, one way is as fast as the other. The Indian did not need any fancy, obtrusive, ugly-looking bow quiver such as is used by modern bowmen. His way was even faster with no unnecessary gadgets in the way. The modern archer is fond of gadgets. He needs glass prisms, peep sights, bow camouflage, balance weights, bowstring markers, arrow glides, and so on, *ad infinitum.* Some even need a "beeper" to tell them when the arrow is at full draw!

I once attended a national archery competition back East. There one could see the finest archery tackle of the day. Most everyone had, in addition, fancy tackle cases, footed arrows, and expensive custom-made bows. But there was one man there who was about as unimpressive a person as I ever saw. He had a five-and-a-half-foot lemonwood bow you could buy in any archery shop at that time for about five dollars, although he did have very good arrows. He had a billed cap on backward and carried his arrows in his hip pocket—no tackle box, not even a belt quiver—but he won the match!

The Indian held the bow loosely; so holding four or five arrows in his bow hand did not handicap his aim or his release. Sometimes for rapid shooting he even held a couple more arrows in his mouth. Modern archers have learned

Reginald Laubin shooting with his Indian "father," Chief One Bull, nephew of Chief Sitting Bull, at Little Eagle, South Dakota.

Kills Pretty Enemy, Hunkpapa
holy man, at eighty-seven years
of age.

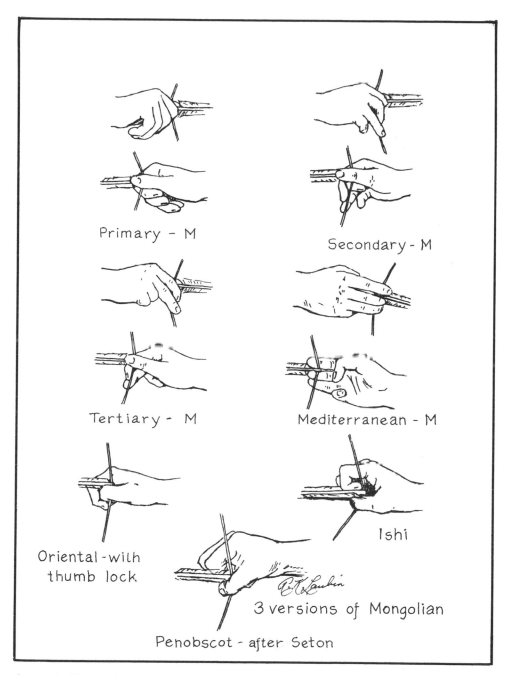

Primary – M

Secondary - M

Tertiary - M

Mediterranean - M

Oriental - with thumb lock

Ishi

Penobscot - after Seton

3 versions of Mongolian

Arrow holds or releases. From Edward S. Morse, "Ancient and Modern Methods of Arrow Release."

that a loose, well-balanced grip is better than a tight, constricted one. The Indian shot instinctively, by concentrating on his target. That is why he found a big target so hard to hit. He did much better, as other instinctive shooters do, when a little piece of paper, an apple, or any small thing was placed on the target so that his mind did not wander to all the pretty outside rings. I understand the *Zen* archer of Japan does something of the same. He does not aim except by concentration. If his thoughts are true, his arrow's flight is true.

A tertiary release like that used by the Sioux but without the little finger on the string, was used by Menominis, Blackfeet, Crows, Omahas, Cheyennes, Arapahos, Comanches, Navajos, Tarahumaras, and Assiniboines, according to Kroeber.[1] We would expect the Assiniboines to use the same release as their relatives the Sioux, but the Cheyenne release demonstrated for me by Mouse's Road was a secondary, or augmented pinch, grip, as I have related. Also my old friend Tahan, a Kiowa, used this same release. Otherwise, both Mouse's Road and Tahan used the same shooting style demonstrated by One Bull and Kills Pretty Enemy. They held the bow overhead, brought it down quickly, pushed it forward and drew the arrow back at the same time, then suddenly released the string, with no holding. Neither of these men were trying to hit anything at the time of their demonstrations. They were merely showing me how they used to shoot.

Standing Deer and Mose Walkingstick, Cherokees, gave fine demonstrations of their shooting at about thirty yards. Their technique was like that of modern archers. They did not hold the bow overhead first as Plains Indians did. Holding a bow thus before a shot in the forest, especially the longer bows used by Woodland Indians, would probably not be very practical. Both were using modern commercial tackle and the Mediterranean release. Standing Deer thought the old-time Cherokee release was a secondary, or augmented pinch, grip. The bows they were using were very similar to old Cherokee bows, about five feet long, but of lemonwood, which was unknown to their ancestors.

I also did some shooting with Blue Bird, a Laguna Pueblo, and Evergreen Tree, a Cochiti Pueblo Indian, but they too used modern tackle and modern technique. I doubt if they did any shooting at home. They probably learned it after becoming "show Indians," although they too were excellent shots at short ranges. Evergreen Tree could group all his arrows in a three-inch circle at twenty yards.

At the New York World's Fair we found Dick Blue Bird running an archery concession in the Seminole village. We had known him for several years. He gave us a big grin when he saw us and said, "I'm Seminole now."

Tahan at ninety winters.

He had a dozen little rubber balloons tied up against a background of bales of hay and charged a quarter for six shots. But business was nil when we came along, and he handed me a bow and a bunch of arrows and asked me to shoot. He thought I might help to get things going again. There was no point in him doing the demonstration, for everybody took it for granted that an Indian could hit the balloons. But the average sightseer did not suppose a white man could shoot with bow and arrow, and most of them hesitated to try. When I broke the balloons one after another people began to collect, and everybody wanted to try it. But I broke all the balloons before I found out that Dick did not have any more! I had to make a dash to the nearest souvenir store to replenish the balloons. Fortunately I did not have to go very far and so saved the day.

Thunder Cloud, an Ottawa friend, showed me a trick that he did at sportsmen's shows. It looked as if he shot arrows right at the people in the audience, and they thought so too. Everyone ducked but no one seemed to know where the arrows went. He showed me how he held three or four arrows in his bow hand (this time with the points down). The arrow to be shot was placed not on the string, but was merely held so it looked to be on the string. This was one case when the arrow was drawn under the first finger of the bow hand; when the bow was released, the arrow was quickly snapped back to lay with the others in the bow hand. Because the other arrows were there no one was quick enough to see what actually happened, and all thought he had actually shot an arrow.

This is rough treatment for a bow and only a very light one with a heavy string should be used for this trick. Even so, I broke a bow "shooting" like this in my Wild Buck Dance on the stage of the Théatre des Champs-Elysées in Paris. I merely mention the trick as part of the instruction I have received from Indian friends.

The Kiowas were famous as archers in former times. In sign language the sign for Kiowa refers to cutting off the right braid of the hair, which they did to keep it from becoming entangled in the bow string. Searching for a picture of an old-time Kiowa, Gladys was delighted when the very first one she came upon was of Zepkoe'eti, Big Bow, Tahan's foster father—the only father he ever knew.

If Tahan could have shot with a bow as well as he could with a gun it would have been something to see. One time he went out with a party of white hunters, and after several hours of seeing no game they all decided to have a shooting match, just to keep in practice. Someone spotted a knot on a tree about thirty-five yards away and bet Tahan he could not hit it. He was carrying a 30/30 rifle; so he took aim and fired. Everyone could see that he hit the knot dead center.

"Pretty good shooting," one of them said, "but it probably was just good luck. Bet you can't do it again."

So Tahan leveled off and shot again. Everyone laughed. "You didn't even hit the tree," they said.

Tahan replied, "Let's go over and see."

They all went over to look, and there was only one hole in the knot. They laughed some more and joshed about Tahan's good luck on the first shot, but he insisted he hit the same spot he had hit before. They all laughed again; so he took out his knife, dug into the tree, and sure enough, recovered two bullets, one wedged right on top of the other! He won his bet and then some. He showed me the two bullets, still practically welded together. He had kept them for souvenirs all those years.

The old-time Indian hunter, before horses were acquired, or when not hunting buffalo, often camouflaged himself by wearing a deer skin or a wolf skin. Even a wolf could ordinarily get closer to his game than a man could. An Indian wearing a wolf skin over his head, shoulders, and back could ap-

Kiowa Chief Zepkoe'eti, or Big
Bow. Notice how the right braid
has been cut off. Photograph
taken by Will Soule between
1869 and 1874 at Fort Sill,
Oklahoma. Courtesy of Western
History Collections, University
of Oklahoma.

proach within twenty to thirty yards of big game like buffalo or elk, making
his kill almost a certainty.

Modern hunters resort to camouflage clothing. If they learn to move
cautiously and noiselessly, there is no doubt that it can help in approaching
game. They even go so far as to camouflage their bows, but with the small,
inconspicuous bow the Indian hunter used, such bow camouflage was unnecessary.

When hunting on horseback some Indians preferred to ride with a pad
saddle, others with a "prairie chicken snare" saddle made of elk horn, wood,
and rawhide, but it seems the majority preferred to ride bareback. Some of
these used a rope or heavy thong around the horse's barrel, through which

they shoved their heels and hooked their toes to give them some support in the tricky maneuvering that had to be executed in singling out their quarry. They also used either a drag rope—a long halter rope attached to the horse's jaw and allowed to lay over his neck and drag on the ground some distance behind— or a similar long rope coiled and tucked in the belt. It was never tied fast to the belt, as this might result in the rider being dragged if pitched from his horse. Tucked into his belt he usually had a chance to hold fast to it in order to retrieve his mount or to let go if that became necessary. One might think that the horse itself would step on a drag rope and stumble or fall, but this seldom, if ever, happened.

In shooting buffalo the animal selected was always approached on its right side. This necessitated the use of a strong bow because the arrow had to penetrate far enough to pierce either the heart or the lungs, and the heart was, as in all animals, closer to the left side. Artists who were really acquainted with Indians like Catlin and Charley Russell portrayed buffalo hunts correctly, but some recent ones, with more romance than fact in their efforts, have shown the rider approaching the left side of the buffalo. I recently saw a sculpture in which the same mistake had been made. What an awkward, ungainly position the archer was in drawing his bow across the horse's neck! One would be lucky to be able to handle a toy bow in such fashion. It is impossible for a right-handed man to shoot even a short bow across his horse to the right with any efficiency.

In war the same tactics were used. The enemy was circled counterclockwise so that arrows or bullets could be shot to the left. A warrior braided a rope loop into his horse's mane and by putting his left arm through it and hanging his left leg over the cantle of his saddle or hooking his heel over the horse's back, his leg through a barrel-rope, he could shoot low over the horse's neck, or even from under the neck, and hardly expose any of his own body to the enemy's view.

On a winter hunt when he was only nineteen years old White Bull shot a buffalo cow but did not place his arrow as well as he later learned to do. The cow was only wounded and turned on him, knocking down his horse as he jumped free. When the horse got back on its feet, White Bull was already astride again and he galloped to within about ten yards of the wounded cow. Before she could charge again he sent another arrow at her. This time it went clear through and stuck in the snow beyond, the cow dropping in her tracks.

White Bull said that on his greatest hunt he killed eight buffalo cows with eight arrows. He thought he might have been able to kill even more, but it was

Indian hunters disguised as deer. An engraving by De Bry after a lost painting by Le Moyne, an artist with the French Huguenot settlers in Florida, 1564–65.

Buffalo hunters disguised as wolves, by George Catlin. From *North American Indians,* by George Catlin.

A drawing of a buffalo hunter showing the old-time Indian way of pointing the arrow to the sky before the bow was drawn and the arrow was brought down on the target. Also shown is the manner of belting the quiver and of holding arrows in the hand.

a very cold day, and his fingers became so cold that he could no longer shoot. He had to stop and rub his hands to warm them. In winter weather it was customary for a hunter to wear leggings, fur-lined moccasins, and an old leather or cloth shirt, but he wore no cap, hat, or gloves. While riding he kept his hands warm by holding them in his arm pits. His horse was trained to turn by pressure of the knees alone. The buffalo robe he ordinarily wore for warmth was left on one of his pack horses because he did not want to be encumbered with it while shooting. Each hunter always had several pack horses which he left behind as he mounted his favorite buffalo runner for the excitement of the chase.

Indians always mounted the off side, or right side of the horse, which came as naturally to them as mounting the nigh (left) side does to the rest of us. In fact, after learning one way, it is difficult to learn the other. The Indians said it was natural to hold the bow and a handful of arrows in the left hand. The right hand was free to grab the horse's mane or the pommel of the saddle (if one was used) to swing up onto the horse's back. To mount in this way it was imperative to mount from the off side. I knew many old Indians who always mounted from the off side, even when riding stock saddles. Our old Crow friend Yellow Brow still rode bareback while in his eighties. When Tahan was ninety-three years old, he rode horseback day after day through his beloved Palo Duro Canyon, recalling memories of his youth seventy years before when he roamed through its mesquite-covered valley with the Kiowas. The young men of recent times imitated cowboys, and I doubt if you could find an Indian anywhere today who mounts from the off side.

Lewis and Clark said that when it was thirty-four degrees below zero nearly half of the Mandan village—men, women, children, with their dogs—went on a hunt of several days duration. Everyone took part in the labor of the butchering, and the meat was divided equally among the families.

They also said that young people shot at marks for beads, which the explorers gave to the best marksmen.

I have never cared much for target shooting as such, but I get as much enjoyment out of roving as any game hunter does from actual hunting. I like to shoot at just about anything that makes a good mark—a distant clump of sagebrush, a stick, a bunch of weeds, a yellow flower, a tiny shadow. A favorite target is simply a milk carton hung on a stick stuck in the ground, or merely placed on the ground. Then, when I hit it, it jumps from its original position and makes a sort of moving target.

I have never been the world's greatest marksman, but I can shoot better with my short bows and short arrows than with the longer equipment I once used. They demand a certain new technique because a twenty-three-inch arrow cannot be drawn to the chin or jaw. Therefore, if one wants to use an anchor point, one must use the heel of the hand instead of the fingers. This does not give as secure an anchor, but with a little practice one will be surprised at the results. Perhaps it may never be possible to do as fine shooting, with consistent results, as with the longer tackle, but the short bows are so much faster, with such a lower point of aim, that they offer more of a challenge and to me are more fun.

As I have already implied, Indians did not use an anchor point anyway, but rather, drew to the chest. For one to become as proficient as I believe some of the Indians were would require starting in childhood as they did. For this reason, I have never been able to completely accept the Indian way, because I started with it too late. I still use the three-finger, or Mediterranean, release which I learned as a boy, and I have changed my anchor, as mentioned, to the heel of my hand at the chin, with the lower joint of the thumb instead of my finger tips, against the corner of my mouth. Many times I do not even use an anchor. With practice anyone can shoot accurately enough for most purposes without an anchor, or even without holding, shooting entirely by instinct with a quick and easy release. Sometimes, just for variation, I do shoot Indian style and amaze myself with some very good results.

When I first became interested in sinew-backed bows, it seemed to me that the sinew would be necessary to prevent breakage in overdrawing a short bow. A six-foot long bow was supposed to take a cloth-yard shaft. Some people thought a "cloth yard" to be thirty-six inches, but I do not believe anyone is big enough to handle a thirty-six-inch arrow drawn to the head.

It was explained to me years ago that cloth was once measured by holding it in the left hand and pulling it to the nose, almost as in shooting an arrow. The average length of this measurement is twenty-eight inches. The full, or linear, yard was measured in the same way but with the head turned to the opposite side, which added an extra eight inches so that our present yard is thirty-six inches, or three feet. Some reports have made a cloth-yard shaft, or arrow, thirty-seven inches, apparently with the consideration that a cloth yard should be different from a linear yard and possibly include extra length for the head. For anyone except a giant even a thirty-six-inch draw is much more than can ordinarily be handled, and the extra weight to give the necessary spine for proper flight of such a shaft would diminish its effectiveness.

South American Indians, of course, make arrows five and six feet long but they do not draw them to the head. They probably think, like many other people, that the bigger a thing is, the better. So a seven-foot bow and a five-foot arrow seem certainly better than a four-foot bow and a twenty-three-inch arrow, even though they have never tried to prove it!

We know now that a cloth yard shaft is really twenty-eight inches, which is an ideal draw for many persons. In the early 1930s the flat "semi-Indian" type of bow became popular. Four inches could be cut off so that a sixty-eight-inch bow could still handle a twenty-eight-inch arrow, with more speed and greater cast. In the same proportion a five-foot bow could handle a twenty-six-inch arrow, which for me was a better draw than twenty-eight. For several years, until my experience with the old Indians, this was the length I used. A four-foot bow, which was about average for a plain wood Sioux bow, could theoretically handle only a twenty-inch arrow. So drawing even an average Sioux arrow of twenty-three inches put quite an extra strain on the bow. This led not only to sinew backing but also to the discovery that bows no longer than thirty-nine or forty inches, backed with sinew, could still accommodate the same arrow.

I have tried twenty-six-inch arrows on forty-eight-inch sinew-backed bows. The bows handle them fine, but finger pinch is severe, and even using the Sioux or an augmented pinch release, the shooting was not as comfortable as when using twenty-three-inch arrows. For accurate shooting the smaller thirty-nine-inch or forty-inch bows with twenty-three-inch arrows also caused too much finger pinch, but this was no great obstacle for horseback shooting. I have found the forty-eight-inch bow with twenty-three-inch arrows to offer no finger pinch, no stack, and perfectly sweet and steady shooting.

Even for an archer afoot these small bows and short arrows offer many advantages. The bow is easy to carry and easy to handle, never in the way. Twenty-three-inch arrows offer no problem of spine. They are perfectly stable regardless of weight or diameter. I have used arrows from 1/4 inch to 3/8 inch in diameter with equal steadiness of flight. Of course the heavier arrows need a higher point of aim; so for this reason I like the 5/16-inch size best. We have made tests for penetration and found that a light arrow from a fast small bow has more penetration than a heavy arrow from the same bow, or even a heavy arrow from a longer, more powerful, but slower bow. This is probably for the same reason that a bullet from a small high-powered rifle has more penetration than one from an old-fashioned large-bore gun.

Catlin and other early observers mentioned the game of trying to keep as many arrows as possible in the air at once—now called the Hiawatha shoot because it is also found in Longfellow's poem. Catlin reported seeing eight in the air before the first hit the ground. This sport required not only great speed and dexterity in handling arrows but also a strong bow with excellent cast to shoot arrows high enough to allow the necessary time before the first returned to earth. My old friend Flying Cloud spoke of an old warrior, Sharp-horn Bull, who could put five arrows into the air. I have managed to get six up, and earlier we quoted a writer who mentioned ten; so I do not think Catlin's story is exaggerated.

The time I got six arrows into the air was the last time I tried this stunt. Gladys was with me, standing just a bit to the left and behind me. I had just let the sixth arrow go when I felt a little jar on the tip of my bow, heard a little click, then a thud and a gasp. When I partially turned around, Gladys looked as if she had seen a ghost and was too frightened to speak. She pointed to a spot between us, and there was the first arrow still quivering where it stuck in the ground. When I pulled it out it was in the ground at least four inches. It had just missed my shoulder and was only a few inches in front of her. From then on I decided if I ever tried a Hiawatha shoot again I would make sure I had a big open field all around me and that I sent each arrow at enough of an angle so that it would have plenty of room to descend well in front of me.

According to Edward Curtis the Atsina, or Gros Ventres of the Prairie, had a Crazy Society whose members, as part of their ritual, stood in a circle and shot arrows up into the air straight overhead, not moving from their positions until the arrows had fallen to earth. This stunt was to display their courage, but I think I could do without membership in that society, even though it would be a less formidable experience than joining the Blackfoot Bear Society, where a new member had to bare his chest and catch a large heavy knife thrown at him from across the tipi in his bare hands!

I suppose everyone who has done any shooting at all has occasionally made an extraordinary shot of some kind. One bright sunny day I took a shot at what I thought was a clump of grass quite a distance away. It looked to me as if I hit it, and I sauntered over to retrieve my arrow. When I was within a few feet of the "clump," up it went with a great whir, startling me no end. It was a sage chicken. The arrow had gone right under him, but he did not make a move until I closely approached him. He had been sitting on it all that time! When I paced it off, I was surprised to find it to be approximately eighty yards.

Another time I was with a group that suggested a new kind of "fast-draw" shooting. I was to place a ten-inch paper pie plate in a split stick, step off twenty-five paces, whirl and shoot. The very first try I put an arrow right through, almost dead center. As usual, everyone said it was luck, which it probably was, and that I could not do it again. But I did do it again, and knew enough not to press my luck too far; I challenged anyone else to do it. Several tried, but no one even hit the plate. You can imagine how well satisfied I was with the day's accomplishment.

Some years ago I met a fellow who had been sent home with a nervous breakdown from the war and had taken up archery as a type of therapy to help him readjust to society. Having been an engineer he went at the thing very scientifically. This was at a time when I was having my first experience with a sinew-backed bow, and we did a little shooting together. His was the first

Tatanka Wanjila "ready for battle" at a parade at Crow Fair, Montana. Photograph from the Laubin Collection.

"scientifically designed" bow I had seen, and it certainly made mine look primitive.

My bow at this time was about fifty-four inches long with a slightly rounded belly, mildly turned-back ears, and lightly sinewed back. It was comparable to some Indian bows I had seen but a bit longer. It had a much lower point of aim with considerably more cast than his, and I outshot him at everything we tried. He could not understand it because he said that scientifically my bow was all wrong. It seems there are some things that cannot be satisfactorily explained scientifically.

I feel certain that anyone who tries short bows and short arrows will find them as rewarding as I have. It is such an ancient variety of the ancient sport that it is now new again and may bring pleasure to many people who are becoming tired of "too much machinery."

## 10

# *Medicine Bows*

One morning Gladys was looking up at the thirty-two bows on the rack above us and began asking questions about them when it dawned on us that up in the loft was a medicine bow I had made, copied several years ago from one in the Peabody Museum at Harvard. Because of the delicate long thin obsidian blade and perishable feathers we had thought it best to wrap it up in a red blanket like a real medicine bundle and store it away. From her inquisitiveness came this chapter on medicine bows.

We sometimes hear of such bows, bow spears, or bow lances and have already spoken of how the Omahas attached a blade to the upper end of a bow so that it could be used in battle as a spear when arrows were exhausted. A number of tribes made such bow lances, but they were seldom, if ever, used as weapons. Usually they were carried as special insignia of certain warrior societies.

Although there were many varieties of these bow lances, they were generally in the shape of a double-curved bow with long ears and a spear point attached to one of the ears. Some of the bows had strings, others did not, but strings were merely ornamental or symbolical. As stated above these bows were not used as weapons. They were truly medicine bows, and although inactive, showed the importance of the bow in the traditions of the tribes using them. All of the medicine-bow societies seem to have come into existence after the coming of the white man and the horse and after the introduction of the use of firearms. The very shape of the bow had symbolic importance, and its power, coming from the thunder, was strong in battle. With the aid of proper ceremonies beforehand the medicine bows were believed capable of blinding the enemy and weakening his fighting ability.

151

Some believe the whole idea started with the Cheyennes.* Certainly the Contraries, who carried bow lances, were famous, but there seems to be some confusion between the Bow String Warriors and the Contraries in some of the literature. The Bow String Warriors (or Soldiers) were a famous organization among the Southern Cheyennes, but they were not the same as the Contraries. George Bird Grinnell in his impressive work *The Cheyenne Indians* does not mention bow lances at all for the Bow String Soldiers, but says they used straight lances. The Contraries did not comprise a warrior society as such, but a Contrary usually belonged to one of the warrior societies and sometimes led it into battle.

Because of the almost repressive responsibility associated with the ownership of a Contrary, or Thunder, Bow the life of a Contrary was not one ordinarily sought after. A person became a Contrary usually through a dream of Thunder, and there were seldom more than three, or at most four, Contraries among the entire Cheyenne tribe. Their bows were associated with the tribal Sacred Arrows, and they had *two* strings, probably because of their "contrary" attributes. Their beliefs and practices were similar to those of the *Heyoka* of the Sioux and concerned thunder and, of course, hail and lightning as death-dealing agents. A number of forms of animal life were involved—the horned lark, swallow, dog, spider, and dragon fly in particular. A Contrary could not own a dog or stay in a lodge where a dog was present. The Contraries did things backward and spoke the opposite of what they really meant to say.

At least three warrior societies among the Lakota, or Western Sioux, had bow lances. My Indian "father," Chief One Bull, was a lifetime member of the *Tokala,* or Foxes, and although he had been a Pipe Keeper rather than a Lance Bearer, he said the Foxes had two bow lances. Most warrior societies had two Leaders of equal rank, and among the Foxes two Pipe Keepers were regarded as of equal rank with the Leaders. One Bull's brother, Chief White Bull, was a Drum Keeper in the Foxes. Their uncle the famous Sitting Bull was a Sash Wearer in the Strong Heart Society; later he became a Leader of the Midnight Strong Hearts, an elite membership within the larger Strong Heart Society; finally he became Leader of the Silent Eaters, a group of twenty of the most important of the Strong Hearts. The Lakota rated the Foxes and the Strong Hearts on a par among warrior societies. One might say that all men of any

---

*The town of Medicine Bow, Wyoming, is said to be on the site where the Southern Cheyennes held their first Sacred Bow ceremony.

important social standing whatever belonged to at least one warrior society.[1]

The Fox bow lances were really lance shafts shaped like double-curved bows with bone points and were the height of a man. They were decorated with strips of deer skin. The grip was wrapped, and at the butt end was a bunch of feathers with an eagle feather hanging from a long string below this bunch. Pieces of fox fur were also tied to the bow curves.

The *Sotka Tanka* (those who stand out like a tall tree surrounded by smaller ones) also had two bow-lance carriers. Their lances really looked like bows with buckskin strings, and they had iron points. They were decorated with white weasel (ermine) skin strips and eagle feathers at each curve and had owl feathers at each end. Little bunches of eagle down were placed along the string.

While all these bow lances were medicine bows and were associated with thunder, the Oglala had a special organization known as the Medicine, or Sacred Bow, Society.[2] In its time it had been a fraternity of exceptionally brave warriors, known also for their generosity and integrity. Four bow lances were used, and this society had only one Leader, who himself was a Bow Owner. Among most warrior societies four lances were used, but they were made in pairs; each pair was different. Among the other societies using bow lances the Bow Owners (or Carriers) were chosen for exceptional bravery, but they were not the society leaders.

Making or even transferring a medicine bow involved a great deal of ceremony, fasting, steam baths, special feasts, "give-aways," and dances. The medicine bows thus acquired such spiritual power that they were afterward treated with the utmost respect and reverence, for they could not only bring good fortune but also might bring calamity if improperly handled. They were carefully guarded to ensure that no woman ever came in contact with them, and when parading around the camp the Bow Men were always in the lead, and no one would dare pass in front of them.

The bows themselves were fastened to straight shafts more than six feet long. To one end of the shaft was fastened a long flint blade. The other end was long enough that it could be set in the ground without the bow touching, for the bow itself was not allowed to touch the ground. There were also four Hanger Carriers who each carried a long, forked cherry or ash stick which was stuck into the ground. The Bow Owners usually hung their bow lances from these hangers. The Bow Owners and Hanger Carriers were supposed to take positions in the front of a fight and never retreat; the bow lances on their hangers marked their positions. Even before hanging his bow lance, if the Bow Owner pointed the blade at the enemy he was bound never to retreat.

These medicine bows were carried with the blade pointing down, and as long as the shaft was carried straight up the Bow Owner was not bound to make a stand. Originally, of course, all spears or lances were used as weapons. However, early in the nineteenth century a new type of warfare developed among the Plains Indians, and lance carriers of most warrior societies used their lances as battle standards, driving the blades in the ground so that the lances marked their positions. Such a warrior was not allowed to leave unless rescued by a brave companion who pulled up the staff. So many lances with villainous-looking blades and all sorts of fancy decorations on their shafts were merely battle standards. The medicine bows were in this category.

The Medicine Bow Society also used the rattlesnake in its symbolism—something almost unheard of for the Sioux. The shaft of the Leader's bow lance was encased in a rattlesnake skin. From the upper end of the shaft (the stone point was at the lower end) hung a buckskin banner, one arm's length, to which were fastened bunches of various-colored feathers, eagle plumes, and tail feathers. A rattlesnake skin was attached near the upper end of this banner. At the lower end of the banner were two eagle tail feathers attached with bear gut, which was iridescent. The Leader also possessed a medicine which would cure snake bites. Rattlesnakes figured also in the decorations used on the robes of the society's officers, and the Medicine Bow warriors wore head bands of rawhide cut in the shape of a snake. The rattlesnake brought bad luck to enemies and gave death-dealing power to the society's members.

The bow lances could be laid on sage or hung on the hangers, and all but the Leader's could be stuck in the ground at their butts, but the bows themselves were never to touch the ground. When the bow lances were put away they were carefully placed in long buffalo-hide cases painted red, and when taken out again the Bow Owners had to take sweat baths and smoke the covers and lances with sweet-grass incense, besides going through other rituals. A long braid of sweet grass was tied to the bow handle for use in making the incense smoke.

All four of the bow lances were decorated with feather pendants at the curves of the bow in the same fashion as those of the *Sotka Tanka.* Some of these feathers were split, dyed red, yellow, or blue, and fastened in little bunches along a braided or twisted buckskin cord. Little buckskin bags of medicine were also tied at the bow curves, and the bows themselves were painted with red zigzags representing lightning, with symbolic red and blue

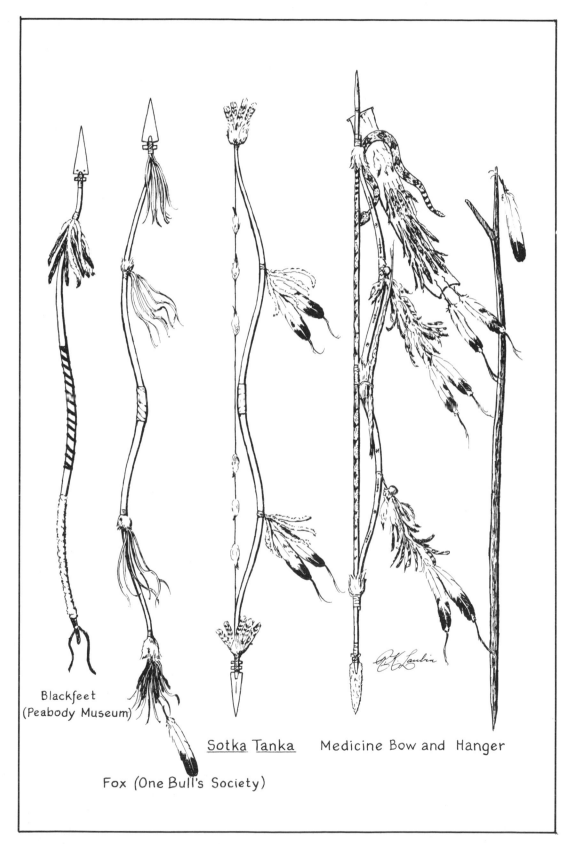

Blackfeet
(Peabody Museum)

Fox (One Bull's Society)

<u>Sotka</u> <u>Tanka</u>    Medicine Bow and Hanger

Sioux and Blackfoot bow lances.

dragon flies, and with spots representing swift-flying insects—all thunder medicine. Feathers of eagles, hawks, magpies, or any swift-flying bird could be used.

The Bow Owners were not allowed to carry or use anything of metal and had to eat from wooden bowls. Officers of the society usually remained in office from two to four years, although they were permitted to remain indefinitely if they cared to. But a Bow Owner was free to resign any time after he had proven his worthiness. He then turned in his bow lance, and the Leader chose a successor.

## 11

# *Indian Crossbows*

Ever so often I have heard references to Indian crossbows, and about equally as often someone asks me if I know anything about them. So I decided to look into this subject for myself. Finally, a few years ago I was delighted when Eldon Wolff of the Milwaukee Public Museum gave me information concerning two Indian crossbows that had come to his attention. The illustrations worked out from his sketches and material concern a Cherokee crossbow, but it is similar if not identical to one from the Potawatomis.

In 1927 a statement was obtained from Chief Simon Ka-qua-dos of the Wisconsin Potawatomis that as a young man he and his companions had made and used crossbows in hunting during the period from about 1862 to 1867. He described the weapon as having a gun-shaped stock with an ordinary hunting bow mounted at a right angle across the stock at its forward end. The stock was grooved, and an ordinary arrow was laid in the groove. The bow was pulled back with both hands, and the string caught in a notch on the barrel from which it was released with a simple trigger device.

It is almost certain that the Indians got the idea of a crossbow from the Whites, but how long ago is a difficult question. The earliest Spanish and French explorers were armed with crossbows, and it is possible that the idea came to the Indians at that early time. Whether they used crossbows for the intervening three hundred years is anyone's guess, but they certainly were not reported in any of the early writings. On the other hand, it is hard to believe that the idea came to them merely as a substitute for a gun, although a gun was a costly weapon to procure and costly to shoot because the Indians were dependent on the white people for everything connected with it. A crossbow could be made mostly from native materials with only a few metal pieces required, as can be seen from the illustrations. Perhaps some white acquaintance, recalling the crossbow of earlier history, suggested it to an Indian bowmaker, who thereupon experimented with the idea and brought it into completion. Certainly the lock is elemental and far different from the locks on European crossbows. It must have been a development stemming from native ingenuity.

There have been occasional mentions of crossbows among the Senecas and other Eastern Indians, as well as among some Canadian tribes, but they have been sketchy and lacking in details of construction.

The drawings show a rather ingenious catch and release on the Cherokee crossbow. The string was drawn back to the catch, or notch, on the barrel under the cap. Before assembling, the dowel was well greased so that it would slide easily. The arrows were similar to those used for a hand bow but fletched with only two feathers; and the shafts were made to fit snugly between the cap and the barrel so that the weapon could be aimed downward if necessary. By squeezing the wooden trigger the dowel was raised forcing the string out of the notch and releasing the arrow. Once a crossbow was described, or even seen at a distance, some such lock could have been a natural development in trying to make the idea of a crossbow functional.

This Indian crossbow must have been somewhat difficult to carry through the forest, and while it may have had some advantage of accuracy over a hand bow, it would have had a much slower rate of fire. But it may have come, too, at a period when the old archery skills were on the wane and was seized upon by some younger hunters who could not afford rifles and who could no longer depend upon their own skills with bow and arrow. It also may have been something of a fad recurring periodically and lasting only a short while each time, but never completely dying out.

It has always been a puzzle to me why there is so much opposition to the crossbow as a hunting weapon. Some of the old prejudices that were prevalent in Medieval England seem to be in evidence yet today. There is no doubt that the war crossbow was a terrible weapon, "too powerful and cruel to use against Christians," but people in those days did not worry much about cruelty to enemies or even to their own countrymen; so the banning of the crossbow must have had other reasons. Crossbows were expensive, and only wealthy noblemen could afford to arm their troops with them. The yeomen were their own commissary and at little or no expense for arms and armor made efficient soldiers. Although the crossbow could nearly double the range of the longbow, its fire power was far slower, and a good archer could send at least half a dozen well-aimed shafts in the time a crossbow could be made ready. The English had

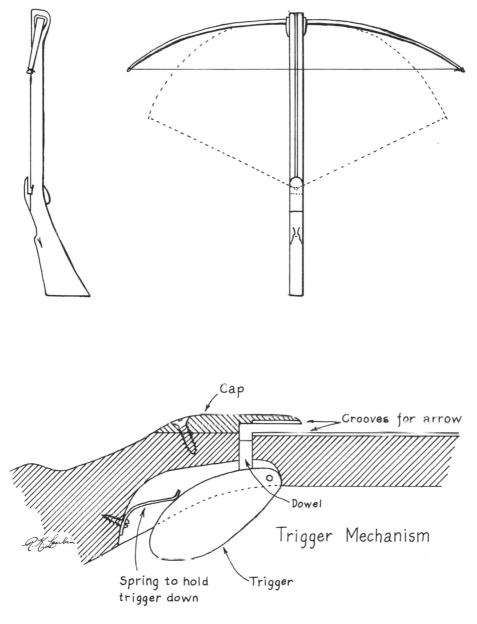

Cap

Grooves for arrow

Dowel

Trigger Mechanism

Spring to hold
trigger down

Trigger

Indian crossbow.

maintained their supremacy with the longbow as their principal weapon and did not want to see it succumb to a "modern" weapon they considered inferior in most respects.

Years ago, when my interest in the longbow was at its height, Gladys and I visited the Metropolitan Museum of Art in New York City, where I was particularly interested in the armor room. There I remember seeing my first Turkish bow and many fine specimens of European crossbows, but nary an English longbow. I asked one of the attendants if they had any longbows.

He laughed and said that of all the priceless articles to be seen there I would ask for something they did not have and that of all the thousands of visitors to the armor room I was the only one ever to ask to see a longbow! Then he told us that there were only two, partially finished longbows in existence and that they were in the Tower of London. They were recovered nearly a hundred years before from a wreck in the English Channel. This English warship had been sunk by the Spanish Armada in 1588 and at that time there were companies of English soldiers armed with longbows. He also mentioned that there was still an English arrowhead imbedded in an oaken door in the Tower and that its point projects on the far side.

Years later I puzzled over the considerable knowledge manifested by this attendant in the museum, but his information was accurate according to later documented material I read.

I can only surmise as to why the longbow nearly became extinct between the time of its military use in England and its revival as a sport weapon in the mid-1800s, but it seems to me that once it was laid aside it was just a stick to most people. To those unacquainted with its romance and history it was altogether too simple, too unappealing in appearance to survive, and within a generation or two all interest and respect for the ancient weapon had disappeared. It was probably used for firewood or otherwise disposed of because it was in the way.

The few who retained an interest in the longbow may have continued to shoot for a few more years out of nostalgia, but eventually the bows must have broken or their owners died, and then their bows sank into oblivion with the others. However, years later a special company of archers, a royal guard, was revived as a matter of historic association, and it is gratifying to know that to this day there is a royal guard of longbowmen that takes part in official functions in England.

The crossbow, on the other hand, was a complicated machine, an expensive article, often of great beauty and intricate workmanship, belonging to the upper classes, and even after its importance as a weapon had waned it was hung on the wall of a great room in the castle as a work of art or as an interesting decoration. Some may still be seen in such positions today. There must be literally hundreds of crossbows still in existence for just such reasons. The first and finest collection of crossbows I have seen is in the Colt arms collection in Hartford, Connecticut. But there are many fine ones in a number of our foremost museums in America and many more to be seen in Europe.

The present argument against the crossbow for hunting—that it is such a silent and deadly weapon—is not entirely valid. Deadly it is, but no more deadly than an arrow from a powerful hunting bow.

I doubt if the Indian crossbows would be much, if any, noisier than an ordinary bow, but all the European-style crossbows I have seen and handled are anything but silent. Of course, they do not boom like a gun, but the rattle and clatter of the release is far more noisy than the twang of any bowstring, and hunters realize that the twang is often enough to alert the game to jump before the arrow strikes. In addition, one shot is all you get with a crossbow, whereas I know many bow hunters who have missed a deer with the first shot and got him with the second. While the crossbow in the hands of most people would be more accurate than a longbow, one must still get much closer than with a rifle, and one shot is all one gets.

The crossbow has been pronounced too dangerous. Its most dangerous aspect is perhaps the fact that it is carried loaded and cocked, but the modern varieties have a safety catch which is practically foolproof and yet can be released instantly when one wishes to shoot.

To me the hand bow is the most sporting way to take game, if one must take it. But since there are still some hunters who use muzzle-loading rifles in their efforts to be good sportsmen I should think the crossbow would rank ahead of a single-shot rifle. I merely make these comments to try to be fair and to help clear up prevalent misconceptions.

A Mohawk Indian told me that when he was a boy he had a single-shot rifle with which he always got his game. Later with a repeater he often missed just because he knew it was not entirely necessary to make a hit on the first shot.

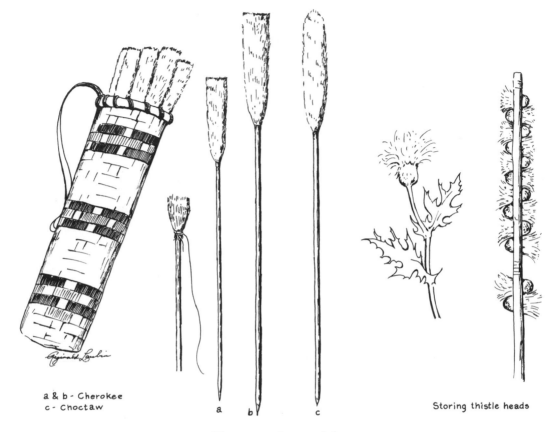

a & b - Cherokee
c - Choctaw

a   b      c

Storing thistle heads

Blowgun quiver and darts.

*12*

# Blowguns, Stone Bows, and Harps

The only relationship between the bow and arrow and the blowgun is that they both use a somewhat similar projectile. The blowgun is an interesting weapon and was known to some tribes of North America. Although it has been reported among some of the Southeastern tribes in rather recent years, some authors contend that it is a latecomer to North America, and also to South America, because it was not mentioned in the early Spanish accounts. They have an idea that it was recently brought to America from Asia by traders, but this could hardly explain how it got into the jungles of the Amazon, how it got to our own Southeastern Indians without being known to others in between, or how it suddenly became so differently developed and changed in appearance. From all the information I have on blowguns of Asia they are usually short, whereas in America they are from six to ten feet long.

North American Indians who used the blowgun did not use poison darts as do the tribes of the Amazon area. The fact that the blowgun in both North and South America has always been used only for hunting and not for war may explain why early writers did not mention it. They no doubt were entirely unacquainted with it. It seems to have been used solely for small game in North America and in the hands of an expert is a very accurate weapon, so that poison apparently was not considered necessary to aid in the killing of birds and small animals.

The blowgun was used until recent times by the Cherokees of North Carolina, and there are still a number of Indians there who are skilled in its use. It was also known to the Choctaws and probably to all the tribes along the Gulf of Mexico, as well as to the Iroquois of New York State, who are believed to have come originally from the South. They used sumac and white walnut for their blowguns, but in the South where the native cane prevailed it was the material used. The Hopis may have had blowguns at one time because even nowadays they blow a feather through a cane tube in some of their ceremonies.

The Cherokees, before having metal tools, are said to have split a long piece of cane in order to remove the solid sections at the joints, glued the two pieces back together again, and wrapped them at intervals with sinew. In more recent times they obtained iron stove pokers which were just the right size for the bore of the blowgun. The poker was attached to a cord, the front end was heated red hot, and then it was dropped through the perpendicularly held cane to burn out the solid sections and make the bore all the way through. The small end of the cane is the muzzle end of the blowgun, acting to some extent like the choke on a shotgun. The Cherokee blowguns average eight feet in length, but I have seen one of ten feet, and they occasionally make a short variety of five or six feet to sell to tourists. I have a blowgun that belonged to Will West Long, a famous old leader and medicine man on the Qualla Reservation.

The Cherokees prefer sourwood for the darts but occasionally use white-oak splints. The splints, of whatever kind, are only about 1/8 inch in diameter and about a foot long, although I have some Cherokee darts for a ten-foot blowgun that are 21 inches long and 3/16 inch thick and some Choctaw darts that are 15 to 26 inches long.

They are "fletched" with thistle down, which is laid on and tied with thread, beginning at the butt end and spiraling down the shaft for three to six inches. The down has to be built up a little more than half an inch in diameter because the breech of the tube averages 19/32 inch and the darts must fit snugly in the breech. The Choctaw darts have five to eight inches of fletching and are left uncut and untrimmed at the butt end. The Cherokee darts, after the down is wrapped in place, are held with the butt against a hot stove lid and burned off flat. A flat rock would have accomplished the same thing in former times. These little darts are beautiful examples of painstaking craftsmanship. When a dart is completely finished, the fletching shows only a little thread at the forward end, and the job is smooth and symmetrical. The business end of the dart is whittled to a sharp point.

Some of the tribes farther south used cotton instead of thistle down on their darts. The thistle down was gathered at the end of the summer or in early fall while still in the heads, and the thistle heads were stored in a split stick for later use (see drawing).

The blowgun is held to the lips as in blowing a trumpet. Both hands are

Cherokee blowgun.

close together with right hand nearest and close to the breech, or larger end, of the tube, not as in holding a rifle. This seems to be the manner of holding the blowgun in the Orient too; so there may have been some connection between the two regions long ago, but not through the exchange of recent traders. The dart is placed in the breech, fletched end toward the opening, of course, and a quick, sharp breath is expelled into the breech of the blowgun. The speed and power of the dart are almost unbelievable. One time when giving a little demonstration in my home for some visitors, and using only my short, five-foot blowgun, I shot a dart completely through a music book twenty sheets thick on the other side of the room. I thought I blew only a tiny puff of air, as the idea was merely to show how the blowgun worked. The eight-foot blowgun I have is far more powerful, and the pressure built up in the longer tube expels the dart with still more speed and force. With it I can shoot a dart a hundred yards or more.

The blowgun can be aimed for line easily enough by sighting along the barrel, but the elevation must be estimated by raising or lowering the tube. With a little practice a high degree of accuracy can be obtained. There is adequate power to kill game as large as a wild turkey, and the shafts will completely pierce rabbits and squirrels.

The darts were carried in a little belt quiver woven of either white oak or cane splints. Colorful designs were included in the weaving by dying some of the splints with bloodroot and black-walnut juices.

The Choctaws are reported to have made a rapid-fire weapon by fastening four or five tubes together in the manner of Panpipes. When these were all loaded with darts, they could be blown one after another in very rapid fashion.

Speaking of blowguns, which use "arrows" but no bow, we might mention another weapon that is a bow with no arrows. I mean a stone bow or pellet bow. I have never heard of such a bow among North American Indians, but it was known in South America and in parts of Asia. It was similar to ordinary bows but in South America was much shorter than the usual very long bow. It was used to shoot, or throw stones or clay balls (pellets). The bows had either a double string, to which a little pouch for holding the pellet was attached near the center, or else a very wide string against which the hunter could hold the pellet for discharge. To prevent the pellet striking the bow, the bow was canted to the right, and the pellet was discharged on the right side of the bow.

Prince Maximilian, writing about his travels in South America, stated that the Indians were remarkably accurate with these weapons and could hit a hummingbird in flight. He said further that they always brought home as many birds as they had taken along pellets, which was some shooting!

The pellet bow was used in Brazil, Bolivia, Paraguay, Uruguay, and Argentina, primarily to obtain birds with precious feathers used for costumes and ceremonies, but sometimes it was even used in war.

Our final tribute to the bow might be for its contribution to the world of music, for it may be one of the earliest of all instruments. Certainly the harp developed from the archer's bow. From the harp came the harpsichord, which in turn was the forerunner of the piano. The violin was originally played with a bow like an archer's bow, and even the present form is practically an archer's bow in reverse.

A number of Indian tribes used a bow as a musical instrument. Long before I knew this I discovered I could play a tune on a bow, fingering it much as one would a bass viol and plucking the string with the other hand. If the lower end of the bow is rested on a board or on a wooden floor, it can be quite resonant. No one who has ever shot a bow can help but notice the tone from

The authors at Crow Fair. Photograph from the Laubin Collection.

the string. In fact, this tone is often detrimental to the hunter because the game may hear it before the arrow can strike. Consequently, various contraptions are used by modern bow hunters to deaden or eliminate the sound. Long before these devices came along some California tribes decorated their bows with little tufts of fur at the nocks, which also served the practical purpose of deadening the twang of the string.

This same twang of the string which hunters strive to eliminate was a note of appraisal to a Sioux warrior. He might even judge the value of a bow by the tone it produced. "This is a good bow," he might say, "It has a good tone," or "This is a poor bow. It doesn't sing well."

Some California Indians used an ordinary hunter's bow as a recreational musical instrument. Such a short bow, only about three feet long, was held straight out, string up, with one end in the mouth, and the string was tapped with the nail of the index finger. By changing the size of the oral cavity they produced an effect something like that of a Jew's harp. (A Jew's harp was originally a *jaw* harp.)

Farther south on the California peninsula the Seri Indians, among the world's most "primitive" people, used a longer bow. They placed the bow, string up, across two overturned bowl baskets which served as resonators, holding the bow at the grip and pressing upon it so that the string changed tautness. By striking the string with a stick they produced varying tones. In this way they could actually play a tune.

So we end on a happy note, even though the old days have gone never to return. We hope this book will help to keep the memories alive and will bring about an interest in another nearly forgotten Indian art.

# *Glossary*

Anchor point—A point on the archer's face or chin to which the bow string is drawn for every shot

Archer's paradox—The arrow bends around the bow and straightens out again to fly to the target as the string is released and returns to its original braced position

Arm guard—A wrist guard, sometimes called a "bracer," to catch the blow of the bow string and protect the arm

Back—The outside of the bow, or the surface held away from the archer

Belly—The inner side of the bow, or the surface held toward the archer

Bow stave—A piece of wood to make a bow

Bowyer—A bow maker

Bracer—*See* Arm guard above

Bracing—Stringing the bow

Cast—The resiliency of a bow; the extreme distance it will throw an arrow

Composite bow—One made of different materials such as wood and sinew, horn and sinew, horn, wood, and sinew

Compound bow—One made of laminations of the same kind of material, such as two different kinds of wood

Chrysal—A pinch, or faulty line, across the grain on the belly of a bow

Crest—Identification marks on an arrow, usually painted rings between feathers

Draw—To draw the bow string its proper distance on a given bow

Ears—The recurved extremities of the bow limbs

Fletching—The feathering of an arrow

Follow the string—The bow partially retains the shape unstrung it had when braced or strung

Foreshaft—A hard wood section inserted in the tip of a hollow-shafted arrow of cane or reed

Limbs—The two bending portions of a bow

Nock—The notches in the bow tips for holding the string; also, the slot in an arrow shaft to fit on the bow string

Point of aim—A point below or above the target at which to aim the arrow point to ensure its striking the center of the target by compensating for its curve of flight

Recurved—The bow tips or ends are bent back, shortening the working part of the limbs and acting as levers to help throw the arrow

Reflexed—The bow reverses itself to some extent when unstrung or relaxed; the opposite of following the string

Relaxed—The bow when it is unstrung and at rest

Release—To let go, or "loose" the arrow; also, the way in which the arrow is held while drawing

Self bow—A bow made of one piece of material, usually wood, but also possibly steel, aluminum, fiberglass, etc.

Shaft—The body of the arrow

Spine—The stiffness of an arrow

Stack—Unpleasant increase in the strength necessary to complete the full draw of a bow

Tackle—All the equipment used by an archer

Tillering—The art of properly balancing the bow limbs and of bringing about a uniform bend through the limbs

# Notes

## CHAPTER 1

1. Alfred Kroeber, "Ethnology of the Gros Ventre," *Anthropological Papers,* American Museum of Natural History, New York, vol. 1 (1907), pt. 3, p. 187.

## CHAPTER 2

1. Edward Gaylord Bourne, ed., *Narratives of the Career of Hernando de Soto* (New York: Barnes, 1904), 1:26.
2. Ibid., 2:68.
3. Ibid., 2:125–27.
4. Ibid., 2:134, 153.
5. George Parker Winship, "The Coronado Expedition, 1540–1542," *Fourteenth Annual Report of the Bureau of American Ethnology* (Washington, D.C.: Government Printing Office, 1896), pt. 1, pp. 329–613.

## CHAPTER 3

1. James Adair, *History of the American Indians* (1775; reprint ed., London: Kingsport Press, 1930), p. 456.
2. Walter James Hoffman, "The Menomini Indians," *Fourteenth Annual Report of the Bureau of American Ethnology* (Washington, D.C.: Government Printing Office, 1896), pt. 1, p. 280.
3. John G. Bourke, "Medicine Men of the Apache," *Ninth Annual Report of the Bureau of American Ethnology* (Washington, D.C.: Government Printing Office, 1892).
4. Morris E. Opler, *An Apache Way of Life* (Chicago: University of Chicago Press, 1941).
5. G. W. Gifford, *Anthropological Records,* vol. 4, no. 1 (Berkeley: University of California).
6. Otis T. Mason, *North American Bows, Arrows and Quivers* (Washington, D.C.: *Annual Report of the Smithsonian Institution, 1893*), p. 640.
7. Mason, reprint edition (Yonkers: 1972), p. 9.
8. Theodora Kroeber, *Ishi in Two Worlds* (Berkeley: University of California Press, 1961), pp. 189–90.
9. Mason, op. cit., p. 45.

## CHAPTER 4

1. Mark Raymond Harrington, *Dickon Among the Indians* (Philadelphia: Winston Co., 1938).

2. See Reginald and Gladys Laubin, *The Indian Tipi,* rev. ed. (Norman: University of Oklahoma Press, 1977), to learn how this is done.


## CHAPTER 5

1. Mason, op. cit., p. 12.

2. See Paul E. Klopsteg, *Turkish Archery and the Composite Bow* (Evanston, Ill.: published by the author, 1947).

3. Meriwether Lewis, *History of the Expedition of Captains Lewis and Clark, 1804-5-6,* ed. Nicholas Biddle (Philadelphia: 1814: reprint ed., Chicago: A. C. McClury & Co., 1902-1903), 2: 450.

4. George Catlin, *Letters and Notes on the Manners, Customs, and Condition of the North American Indians . . .* (London: 1841; reprint ed., Minneapolis: Ross & Haines, 1965), p. 32.

5. Quoted in William P. Clark, *Indian Sign Language* (Philadelphia: L. R. Hamersly, 1885), p. 78.


## CHAPTER 7

1. Philip Stedman Sparkman, *The Ethnology of the Luiseño Indians,* University of California Publications in American Archaeology and Ethnology, vol. 8, no. 4 (Berkeley: University of California, 1908), pp. 187–234.

2. See Alice C. Fletcher and Francis La Flesche, "The Omaha Tribe," *Twenty-seventh Annual Report of the Bureau of American Ethnology* (Washington, D.C.: Government Printing Office, 1911), pp. 16–672.

3. See Peter J. Powell, *Sweet Medicine* (Norman: University of Oklahoma Press, 1969).

4. Frank G. Speck, *Ethnology of the Yuchi Indians* (Philadelphia: University Museum, 1909).

5. Mason, op. cit., p. 181.

6. Frank H. Cushing, "Zuni," *American Anthropologist* 8 (1895).


## CHAPTER 9

1. Alfred L. Kroeber, University of California Publications in American Archaeology and Ethnology, vol. 23, no. 4, pp. 283–96.


## CHAPTER 10

1. For more information on warrior societies see Reginald and Gladys Laubin, *Indian Dances of North America* (Norman: University of Oklahoma Press, 1977).

2. See Clark Wissler, "Medicine or Sacred Bow Society," and Helen H. Blish, "Oglala Sacred Bow," *Anthropological Papers,* American Museum of Natural History, New York, 1:50, and *American Anthropologist* 36 (1934): 180–87.

# Bibliography

Adair, James. *History of the American Indians.* London: 1775. Reprint. London: Kingsport Press, 1930.

Bishop, Maurice. *The Odyssey of Cabeza de Vaca.* New York and London: Century Co., 1933.

Bourke, John G. "Medicine Men of the Apache," *Ninth Annual Report of the Bureau of American Ethnology.* Washington, D.C.: Government Printing Office, 1892.

Bourne, Edward Gaylord, ed. *Narratives of the Career of Hernando de Soto.* Translated by Buckingham Smith. New York: Barnes, 1904.

―――, ed. *The Voyages of Columbus and of John Cabot.* New York: Charles Scribner's Sons, 1906.

Carver, Jonathan. *Travels Through the Interior Parts of North America, in the Years 1766, 1767, and 1768.* 1778. Reprint. St. Clair Shores, Mich.: Somerset Pubs.

Catlin, George. *Letters and Notes on the Manners, Customs, and Condition of the North American Indians. . . .* 3 vols. London: 1841. Reprint. Minneapolis: Ross & Haines, 1965.

Clark, William P. *Indian Sign Language.* Philadelphia: L. R. Hamersly, 1885.

Cushing, Frank H. "Zuñi." *American Anthropologist* 8 (1895).

Elmer, Robert. *Archery.* Philadelphia: 1933.

―――. *Target Archery.* New York: 1946.

Fletcher, Alice C., and La Flesche, Francis. "The Omaha Tribe." *Twenty-seventh Annual Report of the Bureau of American Ethnology.* Washington, D.C.: Government Printing Office, 1911.

Gifford, G. W. *Anthropological Records,* vol. 4, no. 1. Berkeley, University of California.

Grinnell, George Bird. *The Cheyenne Indians.* New Haven: Yale University Press, 1923.

Hamilton, T. M. *Native American Bows.* York, Pa.: George Shumway Publishers, 1972.

173

Harrington, Mark Raymond. *Dickon Among the Indians.* Philadelphia: Winston Co., 1938.

Hoffman, Walter James. "The Menomini Indians." *Fourteenth Annual Report of the Bureau of American Ethnology,* Part I. Washington, D.C.: Government Printing Office, 1896.

Josselyn, John. *New England's Rarities Discovered.* London: 1672.

Klopsteg, Paul E. *Turkish Archery and the Composite Bow.* Evanston, Ill.: privately printed, 1947.

Kroeber, Alfred L. *Arrow Release Distribution.* University of California Publications in American Archaeology and Ethnology, vol. 23, no. 4, pp. 283–96.

Kroeber, Theodora. *Ishi in Two Worlds.* Berkeley: University of California Press, 1962.

La Flesche, Francis. *Omaha Bow and Arrow Makers.* Washington, D.C.: Annual Report of the Smithsonian Institution, 1926.

Le Page du Pratz, Antoine Simon. *History of Louisiana.* Translated from the French. London: 1774.

Lewis, Meriwether. *History of the Expedition of Captains Lewis and Clark, 1804–5-6.* Edited by Nicholas Biddle. Philadelphia: 1814. Reprint. Chicago: A. C. McClury & Co., 1902–1903.

Mason, Otis T. *North American Bows, Arrows and Quivers.* 1893. Reprint. Yonkers: 1972.

Morse, Edward S. *Ancient and Modern Methods of Arrow Release.* Essex Institute *Bulletin* 17 (October-December, 1885).

Murdoch, John. *A Study of Eskimo Bows in the United States National Museum.* 1884. Reprint. Seattle: Shorey Pubns.

Pope, Saxton. *A Study in Bows and Arrows.* University of California Publications in American Archaeology and Ethnology, vol. 13, no. 9. Berkeley: 1923.

Smith, John. *The Generall Historie of Virginia. . . .* London: 1627.

Stalker, Tracy L. *How to Make Modern Archery Tackle.* Eaton Rapids, Mich.: privately printed by the Sherman Printing Co., 1954.

Stemmler, L. E. *The Archery Workshop.* Queens Village, N.Y.: privately printed, 1935.

Tixier, Victor. *Tixier's Travels on the Osage Prairies.* Edited by John Francis McDermott. Translated by Albert J. Salvan. Norman: University of Oklahoma Press, 1940.

Vestal, Stanley. *Warpath.* Boston: Houghton Mifflin Co., 1934.

Wied-Neuwied, Maximilian Alexander Philipp, Prinz von. In *Early Western Travels, 1748–1846.* Edited by Reuben Gold Thwaites. Vol. 22. Cleveland: 1904–1907.

Winship, George Parker. "The Coronado Expedition, 1540–1542." *Fourteenth Annual Report of the Bureau of American Ethnology,* Part 1, pp. 329–613. Washington, D.C.: Government Printing Office, 1896.

# *Index*